Becoming MIGHTY STRONG

Becoming

MIGHTY STRONG

VICKI YOUNG, MH

Strength in God
PUBLISHING

For information contact:
becomingmightystrong@gmail.com
Website: Becomingmightystrongdaily.com

Published by:
Strength in God Publishing

Cover and interior design by Francine Platt • edengraphics.net

Paperback ISBN 979-8-89454-122-8
eBook ISBN 979-8-89454-123-5
Audiobook ISBN 979-8-89454-124-2

Library of Congress Control Number: 2026906431

Manufactured in the United States of America

First Edition

To those in need of healing,
who keep moving forward and
becoming stronger in God each day.

ACKNOWLEDGEMENTS

With deep gratitude to my parents, Ben and Evva Lee Young, thank you for always supporting me in all that I do, and eating my food that I bring up. Thank you for reading the earliest draft of my book in 2022. I feel that Dad is still with me since he graduated from this life in July 2023. Mom, I am so grateful for the support that you still give me.

I am grateful for my brothers and sisters and their families. Everyone is good at making sure that there is vegan food for me at gatherings and glad to see some family members improving their diets and their health.

I am grateful for friends who were there for me when I was at my worst; Susan, Bonnie, Elizabeth, Emily, Sharon, Richard, Stuart, Cheryl, Karyl, and many others. Thank you.

For the knowledge that I have learned from my doctors and other providers, thank you.

I am grateful to Vicki Talmage, for being my first mentor on my natural healing journey.

I am grateful to David and Fawn Christopher and all of the staff at Dr. Christopher's School of Natural Healing, thank you for my education to become a Master Herbalist.

Thank you to those who came to my Natural Healing classes.

I am grateful for Kirk and Kim Duncan and the team at 3 Key Elements. My life has been enriched by your teachings.

I am grateful for Debbie Rasmussen, for the Tuesday author group and all that we learn about writing and life. Also thank you for being my editor.

I am grateful to Francine Platt for designing the beautiful work on my cover and the interior of my book.

A special thanks to Richard Paul Evans; I have learned so much from you. Thank you for sponsoring retreats for authors and future authors. Thanks for having the Author Ready Group.

Dear Readers,

I have been wanting to write this book for many years.

In the summer of 2008, I told a friend, 'I want to write a book and it will be about my journey with Multiple Sclerosis.'

This was during my worst time with my health. Most Monday, Wednesday, and Friday mornings I would go to the MS Exercise Program at the University of Utah and do the exercises that the Physical Therapist had designed for me. I would ride the bus there and back because I didn't have the energy to drive. When I got back home, I had very little energy. I had severe fatigue and brain fog, which affects most people with MS.

In 2008, I was looking forward to the time that I would have the health and energy that I needed to accomplish whatever was important to me. I had the faith that this would happen.

Now, its 2026. For the past ten years, I have had the health and energy that I was looking forward to in 2008. I am now a Master Herbalist; I teach other's the things that they can do to heal their bodies. I have been blessed to help raise children. My journey has been a long one, but it has been so worth it.

My cover has a beautiful sunrise representing each new day that God gives us; a time to draw closer to Him and become a little stronger, physically, mentally, emotionally, and spiritually.

Note: This book is an informational guide. The food, herbs and techniques described are meant to supplement, not take the place of medical advice. For medical conditions, please consult your medical doctor.

TABLE OF CONTENTS

Table of Contents

Trust in the Lord with all thine heart,
and lean not unto thine own understanding
In all thy ways acknowledge him
and he shall direct thy paths.

PROVERBS 3:5–6

FOREWORD

Becoming Mighty and Strong
is not for wimps.

The reality of it lies in the first word, "becoming."

Becoming, signifies more than just a thought pattern,
a new habit, a good idea, and good research.

Becoming connotes that it has not only entered your brain
and soul as more a belief, it is a knowing.
And it doesn't stop there.

The knowing then conjugates to action and practice.
Which means
new thought patterns,
new and different ways of eating and lifestyle choices,
new emotional awareness,
new consciousness of negative thought patterns and
immediately eradicating them,
and replacing them with positive nervous-system-enriching
thoughts and words,
new neuro pathways in the brain…

This is real science today.
This really happens for so many of us.
This is real.

Not only has this "better-way" become
part of your cellular makeup,
it IS your cells,
it IS your knee-jerk choices,
it is your lifestyle, it is who you are, it is what you are,
it is YOU.
It has BECOME YOU.

You don't even have to think about it anymore,
it is the way you do life.

It is the way you do health.
It is the way you do faith.
It is not a path for wimps!

It's constantly "being Tigger"
and getting back-up immediately
and stepping back INTO the daily practice of life and living.

I so appreciate you writing your story Vicki—
my goodness you have walked the walk
and have risen above and overcome, and are thriving.

You have seen the truth and you have had the courage tenacity
and perseverance to not only practice it, but to BECOME it.

The 1938 Westers's dictionary defines perseverance as such:
"Continuance in a state of Grace, UNTIL SUCCEDED
by the state of Glory."

The way to succeed is to keep getting up
and keep moving forward.
The way to fail is to stop and doubt.

This you have done Vicki. And this you are empowering
and inspiring others to do as well. Thank you.

I know this in my own experience and in my own journey
for 48 years
before Vicki met me.
With what I have done professionally now for 45 years I first
began practicing on myself to save my own life; with three
different diagnoses of cancer and a brain tumor removed 15
years ago, and having to learn how to walk again, to talk again,
to communicate and to write again.

What I learned 48 years ago I have been practicing every day
since then, and it is proven to save my life every time.

And not only am I alive,
I am thriving and getting stronger and more healthy every day
thanks to delicious uncooked God-made foods,
my quarterly body cleansing system, enclosed colonics,
fresh Wheatgrass juice every day,
and my Whole Foods daily nutrients.

Coupled with exercise,
Personal study and improvement, service opportunities
and enjoying my beautiful family and my friends;
every day is a new adventure filled with wonder, fulfillment,
love and satisfaction.

I hope you enjoy Vicki's journey.
Thank you for your good writing, and most importantly
for sharing your story and for being such an inspiration
and an empowerment tool for so many of us!

With gratitude and admiration,

VICKI TALMAGE

Vitae health, LLC
vickitalmage.com
vicki@vickitalmage.com
801-420-5225 (text is best)

INTRODUCTION

I grew up in Wallsburg, a small town in Utah. I am the second of six children, I have two sisters and three brothers. I grew up with relatives all around, my grandparents were nearby and aunts, uncles, cousins were all around us. We grew up helping with my grandpa's farm. Sometimes I would drive the tractor as the men hauled the hay. We would move sprinkler pipes. We drank raw milk from the cows that my Grandpa had. We had an apple orchard and a garden. I helped Mom bottle fruit that we would eat throughout the year. We got our meat from the cattle that was raised on the farm. We had all of the equipment to make it into hamburger. We just ate out when we were on family vacations.

I was fairly healthy as a child, I was born with strabismus, my eyes, didn't work together, one of them was lazy. I had surgery on my eye as a toddler but the surgery wasn't perfect, I don't have depth perception. I can see depth because my body adapted and my brain took over what my eyes lacked. When I was eleven I got sick with pneumonia in the summertime. That was crazy to have pneumonia in the summer. I just stayed at home with that bad respiratory illness. I felt bad missing out on activities.

I liked to read, spend time outside and run. I ran cross country (which is three miles) and the one mile and two mile in track in high school.

After high school I worked as a nanny for a year in Rochester New York. I was in the Hill Cumorah Pageant for two years, in 1989 and 1990. I went on a mission for my church to Arkansas, Tennessee and Mississippi. There are a lot of good people in the south but I could do without the humid heat and insects.

I got my bachelor's degree in Community Health Education in 1996.

In 2003, I was teaching CPR and First Aid classes for the Red Cross and working an office job. I decided to go back to school to get a master's degree in Speech Language Pathology. I was single, I had a boyfriend and was helping my sister with her children. Her three children had delays in development and would be diagnosed with Autism. I wanted to help my niece and nephews and other children by being a Speech Language Pathologist. I was working and taking two Speech Language classes a semester to get the classes I needed to get into graduate school. I had a few bothersome symptoms, besides having frequent migraines but they couldn't be too serious, right? Who has time to deal with a chronic illness, I didn't.

By the end of 2003, I had broken up with my boyfriend. In 2004 things started happening that led me to learning more than I would ever want to learn about Multiple Sclerosis. This is my story to becoming Mighty Strong.

THE BEGINNING

"You have MS."

Those were words that I didn't want to hear but I wasn't surprised. After all, for eight months I've been told,

"You probably have MS."

"No, you don't have MS."

"You must have MS, I don't know what else it could be."

I was silent. After several seconds my neurologist. added, "Your spinal tap is positive for Multiple Sclerosis."

January 10, 2005, the first day of the new semester at the University of Utah. And it was raining.

I had just gotten home from classes, when my phone rang. It was Dr. R, my neurologist.

"Your spinal tap results are positive for Multiple Sclerosis. Our specialist, Dr. N will answer your questions."

He transferred me to Dr. N's receptionist to set up an appointment.

One minute ago, it was the beginning of the semester for the new year, now, it was the beginning of my journey with Multiple Sclerosis.

How does one prepare to be diagnosed with a chronic

debilitating disease? There is really no way to prepare for it.

I was busy going to school and working; but I made a decision right there.

I will get through this somehow. This disease is not going to define my life. I will not be in a wheelchair in ten years.

This is My Story

Looking back, I realized that in January and February 2003 I did have medical problems that were symptoms of Multiple Sclerosis.

In January, I started having pain and numbness in my left wrist. I went to Dr. P, my primary care physician. After telling her my symptoms, she suggested, "You have carpal tunnel syndrome. It makes sense with all of your typing at work."

She then referred me to a Work Med doctor.

When the median nerves in the wrist get compressed, it causes progressive tingling and numbness in the wrist and arm and generally leads to surgery. It is a common condition, and my doctor recommended I get a wrist brace to wear. It came with a cloth sleeve, to be worn between the brace and my wrist. The sleeve was supposed to alleviate sweating but it didn't help much. I wore the brace every day for several weeks, but I didn't like how confining it was.

After a while my wrist did start to feel better, however, I wasn't surprised when the doctor told me, "I don't think you have carpal tunnel syndrome."

I didn't think that I had it either; it isn't something that clears up within a couple of months. But the doctor didn't give me any ideas of what could be causing my pain.

While I was working through the pain in my left wrist, my roommate, Susan and I, moved into a bigger apartment. After we moved everything out of our old place, we went back to clean it. The only thing in the living room was a vacuum, but somehow I tripped over it and sprained my ankle.

For a few weeks I had a brace both on my left wrist and on my left ankle. Next, I got sick with bronchitis. This time Dr. P prescribed Zithromax. I took it as instructed and after a few days later, my face swelled up to three times its size.

I couldn't get into see Dr. P, so I had an appointment with my Work Med doctor. She verified that I had an allergic reaction to the Zithromax and explained, "If you take that or any medications related to it, your throat will swell up and interfere with your breathing."

In 2000, I started having frequent migraines. They continued for four years and in April 2004, Dr. P, ordered an MRI of my brain to see what was causing the headaches.

I was fighting a migraine at that time of the MRI, and though I am not claustrophobic, it was a hard experience. I had learned that it's best to keep my eyes closed in that small space. Because of loud noises like hammering, I was about to hear, the technician gave me earplugs.

Now, they give options for listening to music while having an MRI but that wasn't the case back then.

I went to Dr. P to find out the results of the MRI.

"I'll get a picture of the brain," she said. "Then we can look at it together."

I was taking an Anatomy class at the time so said, "We could look at a picture of the brain in my Anatomy book."

She laughed. "I'll get the blown-up picture for us."

She explained the results of my MRI. "Lesions in the white matter of the brain, indicative of a demyelinating disease like Multiple Sclerosis."

This was the first time heard that I might have Multiple Sclerosis, but she couldn't diagnose me. Being a disease of the Central Nervous System, only neurologists can make a diagnosis of MS. She referred me to Dr. L, the neurologist.

This was my first time to go to a neurologist, and I scheduled an appointment with Dr. L at the end of April.

At my appointment with Dr. L, he looked at my MRI and gave me a quick neurological exam. He asked me questions about my migraines.

"How often do you get migraines?"

"At least twice a month," I said. "They can last for two or three days."

"How severe are the headaches?"

"They are very painful. I just want to be in a darkened room with no light for most of the time."

At the conclusion of the visit, he told me, "You don't have Multiple Sclerosis, but I can help you with your migraines."

I didn't say anything when I left, but I had thought.

That isn't right. I do have Multiple Sclerosis.

I didn't know what I was going to do about it, but for now, I was totally focused on finishing the semester. I had an Anatomy final coming up Tuesday evening and I had a lot of studying to do.

The Accident

On Monday May 3, 2004, I was on my way home from work and planned to go grocery shopping.

But that didn't happen.

I was waiting for traffic to clear so I could turn left into the shopping center parking lot. I was rear ended and my glasses fell off. I was aware of everything that was going on, but I felt like I was far away.

The paramedics got me out of my car onto a stretcher and put a cervical collar on my neck. It was so uncomfortable; I just wanted to rest so when I got in the ambulance I shut my eyes.

I heard one of the paramedics say, "I don't think she can open her eyes."

I wanted to show him that I could, and I did, but it was sure a lot of effort. He shined a light in my eyes, I guess to check my pupils.

At the hospital, the x-ray of my neck showed no abnormalities, but I did have whiplash. From the ER I called my roommate, Susan, to tell her what happened and let her know that I needed a ride home.

During the six years that I had my white Mercy Topaz, I had been rear ended several times. It seemed my car was designated to help people come to a complete stop at red lights. Interestingly, my car wasn't damaged any of those times.

I knew Susan didn't drive and couldn't help me, but I thought she could get someone who could. I told her, "I was rear ended and this time my car is totaled."

Maybe it would be nice to get a dark car so people could see it.

Tuesday morning, I called my insurance company. The representative asked me if the rear window was cracked.

I told her, "I don't know because my glasses were knocked off. I didn't get a good look at my car."

Later that morning, a friend gave me a ride to the junkyard. I saw how damaged my car was; everything had shifted. The doors weren't lined up and I couldn't open the door with my key so they pried it open with a screwdriver.

A lot of my important things were in the car, such as my glasses and wallet. I was surprised to find them behind my driver's seat and was so grateful to see that my glasses weren't broken.

The other driver's insurance paid for a rental car for me to use for almost a week. Tuesday afternoon, a representative from the rental car company picked me up and took me to get a car. I got a midsize, the same size that had wrecked. I got it in time to drive to the Trax station and ride up to the University of Utah so I could take my Anatomy final.

What a twenty-four-hour whirlwind before my final. But I did well and got an A in the class.

Getting a New Car

I needed a car and I had heard that a Toyota Camry was a good one.

I would like a Toyota Camry that doesn't cost much money.

I needed a reliable car but I didn't have a lot to spend. My Mercury Topaz had been costing me a lot money in repairs so it would be good to get a better car. On Thursday I got fifteen hundred and fifty dollars for my 1992 Mercury Topaz, then I went to my bank and got approved for a ten-thousand-dollar loan.

On Friday evening, two of my brothers, Rex and Dale, went car shopping with me. We went to the dealership in Rex's green 1997 Toyota Camry. I took a 2000 Toyota Camry, the same color as Rex's car, for a test drive. I really liked it and offered them ten thousand dollars.

"You can take the car home," the salesman said. "If you decide you want it come back tomorrow afternoon and take care of the paperwork."

I wasn't so sure about that, but I took it home.

When we got to my place, I told my brothers, "This is wrong. I'm not supposed to have a car payment."

My brother Dale asked, "So we're taking the car back tomorrow?"

"Yes."

My brothers both shrugged their shoulders.

I felt good about my decision. I somehow knew that things would work out. I didn't know how, but I had the faith that it would happen. I needed a car to get to work and school, and I had return the rental car back on Monday.

My brothers came to get me on Saturday after I got off work.

Rex told me that he had figured out how I could get a car. He had told my two other brothers and parents about his plan. I could buy his car from him for the money that I got from the insurance, then he would get a new car.

If he didn't find a car immediately, then our brother Paul, would let him use his truck to go to work since they worked different shifts. Rex said he had been thinking about getting a smaller car anyway.

He did buy a Toyota Echo that day. It worked out well for him, because when he started dating the girl that he would marry, they were driving from Utah to Idaho a lot.

Rex's car was perfect for me. It was a green 1997 Toyota Camry. It was ironic that the car that I test drove and the car that I got were the same, just different years. It proved to be a great car for me, very reliable for over twelve a half years. The air conditioning always worked, and that was a big plus.

The night after I got my car, my heart was full of gratitude; I was so grateful for my family and what they did to help me.

I hadn't driven it very much over the years, but that was okay. I didn't have car payments or a lot of repairs.

Later, after learning about vision boards, I looked back on this experience. For four days I had been visualizing a Toyota Camry so much in my mind, that I ended up with that car. This was my first big vision board experience without even having an actual board.

The whole ordeal taught me the importance of telling family and friends what I desire so that they can help me reach my dreams.

I was inspired to know that the Camry from the dealership wasn't right for me, that I needed a car without a payment. Being in that car accident was a hard experience, but because of it I was blessed in so many ways. I got a better working car, yes, but the accident eventually led to my diagnoses of Multiple Sclerosis.

The next day was Mother's Day. Rex had left the Camry with me, I had paid for it, but he didn't bring the car title with him on Saturday. My brother Paul took the car title to my parents, and I picked it up there.

I was able to get the license plate and get my car inspected. For a few weeks after the accident, I was in a lot of pain and did not feel like driving very far. Susan was trying to put my new license plate on for me. She was having a hard time because the old one was rusted on. A neighbor, dressed in a suit, came by on his way to a church meeting. He stopped by to see what he could do.

I welcomed his help. "Yes," I told him. "We need to get my license plate on."

He took the old one off and put the new one on. It was a small thing to him, but huge to me.

When I got my Camry, I didn't know how good it would be for me. There were two years, when I was feeling my worst, that I drove less than two thousand miles the whole year, but it was always good to have a car when I needed to go to the store.

My mechanic told me, "Your car needs exercise, it needs to be driven on the freeway."

My brother Paul told me the same thing.

I was planning to go up the canyon to my parents place for Labor Day, and my friend, Bonnie, was going with me.

I asked her, "Will you drive my Camry up to my parents? I have been told by two people that it needs some exercise by being driven on the freeway."

She agreed and drove my car up the canyon and back; my car got exercise.

Recovery

For months, after my accident when I was stopped at a red light, I would look in my review mirror to make sure that the car behind me was stopping. As if that would prevent someone from rear ending me. My body was on high alert to protect me from being injured again.

At times I felt like my entire body was in pain. My neck, all the way down my back, and my arms and legs. Everything hurt. I felt like my new normal was living with constant, chronic pain.

I was taking an evening language development class that summer. I was also working thirty hours a week, going to physical therapy, getting massages, and going to a chiropractor for my injuries.

Classes are shorter in the summer. You are given the same amount of work that you would have for spring or fall semester but given only half the time to do it. It seemed like all the other class members were doing better than me. They were on top of things and I felt swamped. My classmates were at least ten years younger than me. They didn't seem to mind but the chairs attached to the desks were so uncomfortable for me. Many evenings on the bus ride home, it was hard to stop the tears from coming.

One of my big projects was analyzing a toddler's speech. It was due at the end of the semester, the day after the final. Then, about two weeks before the last day, the teacher asked the whole class, "Who can turn their project in a day early, the same day as the final?"

Everyone but me raised their hands. The teacher knew that I was having health problems from a car accident and was fine with me turning in my big project the day after the final. I did get an A in the class; but I felt a lot more stress that semester.

One thing that caused stress was medical bills. My car insurance wasn't paying my physical therapy payments. I learned that even though the car accident wasn't my fault, my insurance would pay the clinic, and then they would submit everything to the other insurance company for reimbursement.

I was getting tired of talking to my insurance company and being told, "They're not billing the right code for us to pay."

Then telling the physical therapy billing office, "They said this is the code that you need to bill for."

It was exhausting. I finally decided to get an attorney. It was a relief to have someone represent me so I didn't have to be concerned about medical bills.

Fall semester was much better than summer. I was working 6:00pm to midnight and taking a class at 7:30am two mornings a week.

My schedule was hard, but I wasn't as stressed. There were times when the pain wasn't so bad and I was learning to live with my new normal. I managed that schedule okay; I would get tired but I wasn't extremely fatigued. I went to physical therapy for the whiplash for about six weeks and then I felt better, but about a month later, my neck was giving me a lot of pain again, so I went back to physical therapy.

At the beginning of one of my appointments, the assistant got me set up on the arm bike and then she went to help someone else. After about five minutes, I felt a sharp pain, like an electrical sensation, shooting down my left arm and I stopped pedaling. I tried to start again a minute later but I couldn't get the bike going.

When the assistant came to check on me, she asked, "Why did you stop pedaling?"

"Because a sharp pain shot down my left arm. There was no way I could continue with that pain."

"I'll get the physical therapist," and she walked away.

The therapist's name was Andrea. "I'm concerned with the pain you're having. I'm going to refer you to a Doctor of Physical Medicine."

I didn't do any more exercises that day. For the rest of that appointment, she massaged my neck and shoulder and put electrical stimulation on it.

That was my last physical therapy appointment. Andrea got me an appointment with a Dr. B. When I met with him I explained the pain that I had been having in my neck, left shoulder, and left arm since the car accident.

He told me, "I think you might have a herniated disc in your neck. I ordered an MRI of the cervical spine, in the neck area."

I knew what he was talking about from taking Anatomy.

On a Friday in October of that year I went to The Orthopedic Specialty Hospital, (TOSH) for the MRI.

I had learned a few things from my first MRI in April. One was to wear clothes without metal in them. I did not want to wear the hospital gown again. I wore a sports bra and sweat pants. Actually, I wore the same sweat pants every time I went to get an MRI for many years. The machine was just as loud and claustrophobic as I remembered. I'm glad that I'm a small person, the MRI bed is very narrow.

This time, at one point, the MRI technician told me not to move.

"Sorry, I didn't know that I was."

The brace around my head and neck made it hard to move. Before I left, the MRI technician checked to make sure that all of the views of my cervical spine looked good. But even so, the MRI department called me on Monday.

"Vicki we need to do your MRI again."

"Really? I don't want to go through that ordeal again."

"I know, I'm sorry. The radiologist saw something on your MRI and we need to check into that."

"Can you tell me what's wrong?"

"No, I can't. But can you come in today?"

"Yes, if I have to. I guess I can work it in my schedule." I was able to go in between classes and work.

Now I should be good at getting an MRI, my third in about six months and just three days from having my last one. They did everything that they had on Friday. Then they put what they called contrast in a vein in my arm and took some more views. The contrast is a dye called gadolinium. It gives the doctor a better view of different areas.

Two days later I had an appointment with Dr. B.

He said, "I wonder why they did the MRI a second time and used contrast. I don't need that to look at a herniated disc. I hope that they don't charge you for both MRIs."

"My car insurance should cover the cost of the MRI," I assured him. Which is what happened.

It's nice to have a doctor who is considerate of me having to pay for this expensive procedure.

Then he read the results to me. "There are lesions in the white matter of the cervical spine which could indicate a demyelinating disease such as Multiple Sclerosis. That's why they used contrast the second time. They had seen the lesions from the first MRI and using contrast, showed them if the lesions are recent."

I sighed. "I have heard before that I might have Multiple Sclerosis. In April, I had an MRI and was told that it showed lesions in the white matter of my brain, which could indicate Multiple Sclerosis. But the neurologist that I went to, Dr L, said that he didn't think I had MS."

So, I got an appointment with Dr. L to show him the results of the MRI of my cervical spine. When he saw them he didn't think it was significant enough to diagnose me with Multiple Sclerosis. Like before, he didn't give me a neurological exam like I came to expect with a neurologist that specializes in MS. Dr. B, referred me to Dr. R, a neurologist that he knew.

My appointment with him was December 29th, more than two months away. It would have been nice to have the appointment sooner but I was also glad that it was after Christmas and after the semester was over.

The Diagnosis

I was nervous when I went to my appointment with Dr. R. His physician assistant, Jane, met with me first.

She asked, "How often do you get migraines?"

"At least twice a month and they last for days."

"What other neurological symptoms are you having?"

"I've been feeling dizzy a lot the past few weeks. My left arm hurts and my hand and fingers are tingly. My left foot hurts too but not as bad as my left arm."

She did a neurological exam. Most of my reflexes were good

except for the bottom of my feet, especially my left foot. She had me hold out my arms in front of me; she told me she could see a tremor in my hands.

I hadn't noticed that.

She shined a light in my eyes; she said it was to check my optic nerve. It was fine. Then I was asked to walk across the room, and also to walk heel to toe.

Dr. R came in and looked at my MRI scans. He did a neurological exam, checking my reflexes and strength. "From the results of your MRI's and neurological exam, I think you have MS but I'll do a spinal tap to make certain." Then he explained, "When I do the spinal tap, I will use a long needle."

He paused for a few seconds then asked, "Do you have any questions?"

"No." Actually, I did have a lot of questions, I just was so overwhelmed I didn't know where to start.

I went to the receptionist to schedule the spinal tap.

"The next available time for Dr. R is Monday January tenth."

"I can't do that day, it's the first day of Spring semester. A Friday would be better for me."

She called me later. "I scheduled you for a spinal tap on Monday January third. Will that work for you?"

"Yes, that works for me."

I got an appointment sooner than I thought I would.

The receptionist continued, "Someone needs to give you a ride. You cannot drive after a spinal tap."

In some ways it seemed like everything was happening fast. I was going to be diagnosed with Multiple Sclerosis and my being super busy wasn't going to stop that. It was time for me to learn more about this disease.

Rich, a representative from my church suggested, "Call my friend Marilyn. She's had MS a long time. She can tell you about it."

I did call Marilyn.

"I was diagnosed with MS twenty years ago," she said. "Neurologists have learned a lot about it since then. There were no medications to treat MS in the 1980s. Injectable medications were developed in the 1990s, and there are no pills to treat it. I use a cane; I get tired easily but I still do a lot."

I was glad to talk with someone who had lived with MS for a long time but still doing okay.

I told her that my only experience with people who have MS was when I worked as a CNA in a nursing home in 1996. There were two ladies with it; one was in a wheelchair, the other one was bedridden and couldn't use her arms or legs.

That's the only reference I had.

When the day came for my appointment, a friend from my church gave me a ride to Dr. R's office.

Spinal Tap

A lumbar puncture, or commonly known as a spinal tap is a medical procedure, where the doctor inserts a needle in the space between two lumbar vertebrae, which is in the lower back. A spinal tap is used to diagnosis infections like meningitis, and Multiple Sclerosis and other conditions of the Central Nervous System.

Before I had my spinal tap, I heard people who had the procedure for meningitis talk about it being the most painful procedure that they had ever done, I also heard that drinking a lot of water twenty four hours before the procedure will relieve the painfulness. I drank a lot of water the day before I had the spinal tap and it wasn't very painful for me.

When I arrived for my appointment, the first thing that they directed me to do was to have my blood drawn. The phlebotomist put my blood into eight to test to see if I might have anything that has similar symptoms, such as Lupus. That looked like a lot of blood.

He jokingly said, "Now that I have taken all of your blood, you can get the spinal tap."

Dr. R's physician assistant Alisa did my spinal tap. She had me lay on my side on a table, my knees were bent up to my chest. I didn't even need to take my clothes off. I just pulled my pants down so she could access my I back. She used a large needle to puncture the lumbar area between the vertebrae and a syringe to collect the cerebral spinal fluid. They are looking for some proteins that show abnormalities in the immune system.

After the procedure was completed, I laid down in a dark room for an hour, the start of the twenty four hours laying down. When it was time to go home a nurse pushed me in a wheelchair to my friend's car. She laid the front passenger seat all the way down so that I would be laying down on my way home. People are prone to getting a terrible headache after a lumbar puncture, laying down for the day, prevents that and it also prevents leaking of the cerebral spinal fluid. I was fine in my recovery from the spinal tap.

Another friend thought that since I had to lay down all day, then it would be a good time to have a Jamba Juice smoothie. She brought me a strawberry smoothie, that tasted so good.

*Look unto me in every thought,
doubt not, fear not.*

DOCTRINE AND COVENANTS 6:36

LEARNING TO LIVE WITH MULTIPLE SCLEROSIS

I had a lot to learn about living with Multiple Sclerosis. The most important thing that I wanted to know was how this chronic disease was going to affect me? But that wasn't something that anyone could tell me. I was hoping I could still work for the next twenty years.

But that didn't happen.

Multiple Sclerosis is an autoimmune disease, where the immune system attacks the protective insulation of nerve fibers, known as myelin, causing a buildup of plaques and then scarring and hardening of multiple nerve fibers. This process is referred to as sclerosis. You can have different symptoms depending on where the sclerosis occurs, such as in the brain, spinal cord or optic nerve.

Doctors do not know exactly what causes Multiple Sclerosis. There is research showing that previous exposure to Epstein-Barr virus can contribute to getting a diagnosis of Multiple Sclerosis. It can be dormant in your body for twenty years and then manifest as MS.

When my mom heard this, she told me, "You had pneumonia in the summertime when you were eleven. No one else in the family got it."

Multiple Sclerosis is more prevalent the farther you live from the equator. Doctors think this has to do with lack of sun exposure, so your body doesn't synthesize vitamin D from the sun. When you get your blood tested for your vitamin D level, normal is between thirty to eighty. It's better for people with Multiple Sclerosis and other immune diseases to have over fifty on the scale.

Many people are diagnosed with MS after being in a car accident, as it can often trigger symptoms. MS affects people as young adults in the prime of life; most are diagnosed between the ages of twenty and forty. I was thirty-four, almost thirty-five so I fit right into that age group. Three times as many women than men are diagnosed with MS, which falls into line with all auto immune diseases having about three times as many women than men.

I don't have any relatives who have MS, but there does seem to be a genetic component. People who have a parent or sibling who has MS are more likely to be diagnosed.

The risk of someone in the general population getting MS is .01%. The risk of a child with one parent who has MS is 2%. The risk of a child with two parents who have MS is 12.2%. The risk for a sibling is approximately 5%. The risk for grandchildren, cousins, nieces and nephews is 1% (National MS Society website)

People who live in an area with a low incidence of MS and then move to an area with a high incidence of MS are more likely to be diagnosed. This shows that there is a lifestyle component. Over the years, I learned that I could change my lifestyle and improve my health to decrease my symptoms.

In order to be diagnosed with MS, you need to have lesions in more than one area of the Central Nervous System(CNS) or have more than one lesion in the same area. At the time I was diagnosed I had lesions in my brain and cervical spine.

I was diagnosed with Relapsing Remitting Multiple Sclerosis, the most common form.

The relapsing part is worsening symptoms and the remitting part is when the symptoms improve and go away for a time. Secondary Progressive Multiple Sclerosis generally starts out as Relapsing Remitting Multiple Sclerosis but then the disease progressively gets worse without much remitting. In Primary Progressive Multiple Sclerosis, there are worsening neurologic symptoms from the onset. Clinical Isolate Syndrome (CIS) is a first episode of neurologic symptoms caused by inflammation and demyelination in the Central Nervous System. The incident, which must last for at least twenty-four hours, is like MS but doesn't meet the full criteria. People with CIS may or may not go on to develop MS. When CIS is accompanied by lesions on a brain MRI that are similar to those seen in MS, the person has a high likelihood of a second incident of neurologic symptoms and diagnosis of Relapsing Remitting Multiple Sclerosis.

Medications that affect the disease course of MS are known as disease modifying medications. At the time I was diagnosed with MS, there were only four FDA approved medications for Relapsing Remitting Multiple Sclerosis and they were all injectable. The four medications were Avonex, Betaseron,

Copaxone and Rebif. A few years later, Tysabri, an IV medication was approved by the FDA. There weren't any medications approved for the other types of MS. Now there are nine injectable medications, nine oral medications and four infused medications (By the time you read this, there might be a few more medications approved for MS). Some of these medications are approved for CIS, some people with Secondary Progressive MS, will continue with the medication that they have been taking. Recently, I saw that an oral medication for MS costs over eight thousand dollars a month, which is more than any of my injectable medications or IV medication cost. (From MS Website)

When I went to Dr. N's office, I first met with his physician assistant, Emily. She did a neurological exam, checking the strength of my arms and legs, and the sensation in different parts of my body by how well I could feel a pin prick. She pointed out a tremor in my left hand.

Then Dr. N came in and did a neurological exam. "You need to exercise regularly and take Copaxone. It's an injectable medication that is to be taken every day. Exercising and taking Copaxone will stop your MS from progressing."

His office assisted me in requesting that my insurance cover Copaxone. The chemical name of Copaxone is Glatiramer Acetate which is a synthetic protein that stimulates myelin basic protein, a component of the myelin that insulates nerve fibers in the brain and spinal cord. This medication seems to block myelin damaging T cells through a mechanism that is not completely understood. (Copaxone prescribing information)

Taking Copaxone

I received a letter that my insurance approved Copaxone for me at the beginning of February. It was shipped to me in a box with a Styrofoam protection and some ice packs to keep the medication cold.

On February 9, I had an appointment with Emily to show me how to inject the Copaxone. It came with an auto injector to put the needle in so I wouldn't see the needle as it goes in the skin.

A planner came from the manufacturer with the Copaxone. It was to keep track of where I gave myself an injection each day. There are seven different areas on the body to inject Copaxone, so you can use the same place each day of the week. The different areas of the body are the abdomen, two inches away from the belly button, fleshy part of the hips, top outer part of the thighs, and the upper outer arms. When she walked me through it the first time, I injected into my abdomen.

The instructions were to take the Copaxone prefilled syringe out of the fridge at least twenty minutes before injecting so the medicine is at room temperature. I cleaned the area with an alcohol wipe, then let my skin air dry completely before injecting. I put the syringe into the auto injector. I liked having that so I didn't have to see the needle.

I wasn't used to getting shots. When I gave myself one it was very painful. After a while the pain wasn't just from the needle. For about a month I was having a hard time injecting myself. The process should have taken five minutes but it was taking me about twenty.

Do I have to inject myself every day? Did I have to have one on my birthday?

I did have an injection every day but a few times my room-mate helped me. She gave me my injection on my birthday.

One morning, as I was gathering the strength to take my injection, I felt love from my Savior; like His arms were wrapped around me. I received the message that He knew what I was going through. He had gone through this before me.

I can do this and I will be okay.

In the Book of Mormon, Alma 7:11 says, *"...He will take upon Him the pains and sicknesses of His people."*

Jesus understands everyone's struggles in a way that no one else can. Remember, that through His Atonement, He can strengthen each of us in our unique struggles.

After that experience, I could quickly give myself a shot in about five minutes. I went to a meeting sponsored by the manufacturer of Copaxone.

A speaker said, "When you're giving yourself a shot don't think about anything, just like when you are brushing your teeth, you aren't thinking about anything."

Well, at least I'm not having a lot of pain when I'm brushing my teeth.

I told some friends that I had just been diagnosed with MS. We had been in a singles ward together at our church. They told me that three or four years earlier one of our friends, Tammy had been diagnosed with MS. I knew her but I didn't know that.

They invited me and her over for Sunday dinner.

It was good to talk with Tammy. She had been diagnosed with MS several years earlier and it helped me to hear her experiences. She was also taking Copaxone. While the others were cleaning up after dinner, she answered some specific questions that I had about taking the medication.

I signed up with the National Multiple Sclerosis Society's Knowledge is Power Program. They sent out information about a different topic each week for eight weeks.

1) What is Multiple Sclerosis?

2) Dealing with your Diagnosis

3) Working with your Doctor

4) Treatments in MS

5) Disclosing your Diagnosis

6) Disease-Modifying Treatments for MS

7) The Impact of MS on the Family

8) Maximizing Your Employment Options

It was good to get tips about dealing with my diagnosis, that everyone goes through stages of grief with being diagnosed with a chronic disease like Multiple Sclerosis.

It was good to read about disclosing your diagnosis to employers, my rights under the Americans With Disabilities act (AD), and getting on intermittent FMLA, which I was needing to use the intermittent FLMA, soon after getting this information.

I had been taking Copaxone for a few months when I traveled to Los Angeles, California with my vials and the autoinjector. I was going to visit my cousin, a Speech Language Pathologist. In her profession she went to homes of preschoolers to work with those who had speech problems. She made arrangements for me to go with her for a few visits. I enjoy spending time with children and thought that working with preschoolers or in an elementary school would be good for me.

I had hoped to get into the same profession as she was; Speech Language Pathologist.

In the Spring, I participated in the MS walk with several friends from church. Then, I ran a 5K race in the Sugarhouse Park in October of 2005. I was glad that I felt up to doing that. I didn't run as fast as I had in high school but I did okay.

I took Copaxone for fourteen months. I went to educational classes sponsored by Teva, the manufacturer. These classes were held at hotels; they provided a meal for those with MS and their guest.

Someone with the disease was a spokesman for Copaxone and would tell about their experiences. A neurologist would speak about the ongoing research.

At these gatherings, I visited with people at my table. I was surprised to often hear several people say, "Someone injects it in my arm for me since I can't see to do it myself."

I shrugged. "I look in the mirror to inject in my arms, just like you look in the mirror to wash your face and put make up on."

One of them commented, "Oh, that is something to try."

At one of these classes I heard one of the neurologists say, "Some of my patients take Copaxone every other day and are doing fine."

I had been diligently taking Copaxone every day for over a year because my neurologist told me, "If you take Copaxone and exercise every day then your health will improve."

I would frequently walk outside or on a treadmill. My health was not improving. During the fourteen months that I took Copaxone, and after hearing the neurologist say that some of his patients only take Copaxone every other day; one busy day I didn't give myself an injection. I realized that I had forgotten.

That's okay, it isn't helping me anyway.

An attorney in my church told me that someone at my work has Multiple Sclerosis. He suggested I come and visit with her. I did that. Her neurologist is also Dr. N, and she gave me a few ideas.

TIP: It is important to turn to people to give you advice, who have gone before you. That is especially important when you're newly diagnosed with a chronic disease. At this point, I teach people who have been diagnosed with Multiple Sclerosis, things they can do naturally to improve their health.

In April 2005 I had issues with my bladder, causing me to have a relapse. A nurse came to my place to give me Solu-Medrol, an IV steroid which is used to treat an acute exacerbation in Multiple Sclerosis.

I took it over the weekend. The IV needle stayed in my right arm the entire time and the nurse put in the steroid for a few hours each day. I was self-conscious about going to church with a bandage covering the IV needle on my lower arm, so I wore a white sweater and no one noticed it.

I had an MRI of my thoracic spine. It showed lesions so then I had them in the brain, both areas of the spinal cord, the cervical, and thoracic spine.

Changing Neurologists

Dr. N wasn't working out for me. He had a bad bedside manner and he wasn't understanding. I needed a neurologist who was sensitive to my needs. It was interesting to me that he told his patients to exercise but he didn't do that himself. He was obese and suffered from diabetes. I prefer people who I go to for advice to do what they tell others to do.

I got an appointment with Dr. F in February 2006. He is another neurologist in the Salt Lake City area who specializes in Multiple Sclerosis.

The first time I saw Dr. F, I had a lot of paperwork to fill out about my symptoms. He did a thorough neurological exam and tested for evidence of weakness by asking me to resist as he pulled or pushed my arms or legs.

I was weak.

My coordination was tested by touching my nose with my index finger and then touching his index finger back and forth and then doing that with the other hand. My tremor showed prominently doing the finger to nose test. He had me stand still with my eyes closed to test my balance. That was hard.

I also did the tandem walk, also known as heel to toe walk, which is placing the heel of one foot directly in front of the toe of the other foot and walking in a straight line. That is challenging. He also checked how I walked with a regular gait. He had a large exam room so there was plenty of space to do the walk tests.

Sensory changes are tested in a few ways. With my eyes closed, he moved my toes and fingers in different positions, I said if they were up or down to see if I could tell where they were in space. He used a gentle pin prick to test changes in skin sensation.

He told me to, "Follow my finger," to test my eyes. Then he asked, "How many fingers am I holding up?"

"One, I know that it looks like I see double because my eyes don't work together. I was born with strabismus. I had surgery to correct it when I was a year old but that surgery wasn't perfect so my eyes still don't work together, but I can still see fine.

I've had other issues with my eyes, but many people with MS have lesions in their optic nerve. I'm grateful that I have never had those particular lesions.

I did tell Dr. F "that I have frequent migraines."

He told me that he just treats Multiple Sclerosis, and that he would refer me to a neurologist at the Salt Lake Clinic to help control my migraines.

I learned that neurologists specialize. The first neurologist that I went to Dr. L, didn't specialize in Multiple Sclerosis, I think that he should have referred me to a MS specialist, especially when I had my second MRI with, "lesion indicative of a demyelinating disease like MS. I don't know what Dr. R's specialty was, or if he treated a wide range of neurologic disorders and would refer to a specialized neurologist when needed. After I started going to Dr. N and attending MS meetings, I heard about two other neurologists in the Salt Lake Valley who specialized in Multiple Sclerosis. For a while I was going to two neurologists, one who specialized in MS and the other one specializing in migraines and other headaches.

My friend, Susan has a sleep disorder called narcolepsy. For many years she went to a neurologist who specialized in sleep disorders, narcolepsy, insomnia and sleep apnea, that was in the same building as Dr. N.

My cousin's little boy was born with a rare neurological condition. He saw pediatric neurologists at the Primary Children's Medical Center.

I don't know what Dr. R's specialty was, or if he treated a wide range of neurologic disorders, but I hoped he would refer me to a specialized neurologist when needed. After I started going to Dr. N and attending MS meetings, I heard about two other neurologists in the Salt Lake Valley who specialized in Multiple Sclerosis. For a while I was going to two neurologists, one who specialized in MS and the other one specializing in migraines and other headaches.

Dr. F ordered an MRI of my brain and my cervical and thoracic spine, which I had in early March at LDS Hospital. I had the brain MRI on Wednesday and the cervical and thoracic spine MRI together the next day. A friend from church gave me a ride to my MRI.

To have the cervical and thoracic spine MRIs together meant that I was in the MRI machine for a very long time. That was hard on my body to be in that narrow, cramped area for what seemed like forever. When the MRI was over and the technician was helping me off the narrow bed of the machine, I asked, "What time is it?"

"It's 11:30."

"I was in here for two and a half hours? Wow, no wonder it felt like forever."

I had a relapse at that time and I got IV Solu-Medrol in Dr. F's office. I started to have severe fatigue. I wished that my health wasn't deteriorating when I first met Dr. F, but I'm sure he was used to that. Dr. F was my doctor for over eighteen years. I had found a good neurologist who worked well with me. I learned recently that he is retiring.

Tip: Find great doctors and other providers to be on your health care team, who understand you.

School

It was 2006, and I would have preferred to be getting ready to go to graduate school to become a Speech Language Pathologist. But instead of asking my professors for recommendations to Graduate School, I had to tell them, "I will not be going to because I have Multiple Sclerosis and the fatigue is just too much."

They were disappointed to hear that I wouldn't be going on.

One of my professors told me, "You're too smart to not go to graduate school."

That's what I really wanted to do. I know that a lot of people have missed opportunities after being diagnosed with chronic conditions. That was disappointing to me.

Employment

I told my supervisor right after I was diagnosed with Multiple Sclerosis, but there is a debate about whether you should tell your employer. Some people feel a certain degree of embarrassment or fear of being fired.

In April, I had a relapse and I was on IV steroids for three days. I missed a day of work.

When I told my supervisor, she said, " You need to get on FMLA so that won't be counted against you."

I got the FMLA paperwork from the HR department, then went to my doctor to have him sign it. Luckily, that day in April when I missed work was retroactively covered.

After I was on FMLA, if I couldn't go to work because of MS symptoms, or I needed to leave early then I could, without it affecting my attendance.

In the early part of 2006, I started feeling worse. Severe fatigue and brain fog returned. I was off work for four weeks, from the early part of April into May and then I worked part time for a month with a note from Dr. F.

I was so grateful that I had short term disability. Being on FMLA allowed me to take some time off when I wasn't able to work and the short-term disability paid me for that time off.

I tried taking medicine to combat the fatigue. This was the first time that I had ever taken anything to give me energy. Many people take caffeinated drinks such as coffee, soda pop, or energy drinks to get them going at the beginning of the day. I had never done that. But there wasn't any medication approved for MS fatigue.

Dr. F prescribed Provigil, which is approved for those with the sleep disorder, Narcolepsy. It is very costly, over five hundred dollars a month, so my insurance denied it. Then Dr. F prescribed Amantadine for my fatigue, an approved anti-Parkinson medication and is sometimes prescribed for MS fatigue. It is inexpensive so my insurance approved it. Amantadine has a side effect of dry mouth. After I was on it for a couple of weeks, I realized I'd had a cough for about as long as I had been taking Amantadine. I decided to stop taking it to see if I would stop coughing—that is exactly what happened.

Just to make sure it was the medicine that was making me cough, I started taking it again, and right away I started coughing. I decided that I would never take Amantadine. If it was helping me combat the fatigue in some ways, that was done away with when I would lay down and start coughing instead of going to sleep.

After a few months, my insurance approved me to take Provigil and I took it for two and a half years. I was taking a higher dose than most people but it really didn't help me.

In 2006, I was working the 11:00-7:30 shift and had a new supervisor. He wasn't familiar with the reason that I was first got on FMLA. He didn't ask and he didn't need to know, but he did look out for me. There were three other people on my team who were on FMLA.

At times my supervisor would announce mandatory overtime. One of the others who was on FMLA would get upset because she couldn't work it. I would be quiet because I knew that the overtime didn't apply to me, or the others who were on FMLA.

That's what our supervisor would say.

During this time, I had a note from a medical provider, 'While at work, Vicki should take a five-minute break every hour." Once I reached the time limit for breaks then I would log out and then log back in. I was scheduled to work forty hours a week. A lot of weeks I had a hard time working just thirty hours.

One day in July I got to work and my supervisor told me. "The AC is not working, you can go home since you have FMLA."

I so wanted to work that day but there was simply no way I could. I went outside to go home and the ninety-degree weather felt better than inside the hot building because there was a little breeze. When I went to work the next day, some of my coworkers had said they got headaches from working with no AC all day.

Going On Disability

In the middle of August 2006, I had an appointment with my Primary Care Physician before I worked, After the appointment, I felt drained, like I just couldn't do one more thing. I called in FMLA. I never went to work there again. I let my disability insurance know that I needed to be on long term disability and I made an appointment to apply for Social Security Disability.

I had been paying for short- and long-term disability as some of the benefits at work. I am so grateful that I had that and I encourage everyone to get short- and long-term disability coverage. Many people get an injury or illness that prevents them from working for 3-6 three to six months, and then there are other people like me who are on disability for ten years or longer.

My disability insurance paid me sixty percent of my income and I also got medical insurance, the same as I had been getting through my employer for two years; making it so I didn't have to go on COBRA. It was good insurance with minimal copays for most services, not a high deductible, like many plans are now.

My neurologist, Dr. F, sent my medical records to the local Social Security office in September. I went for my appointment to apply for Social Security Disability. I knew I would likely need an attorney, so I went the National MS society, and was referred to an attorney's office to assist me in applying. It didn't take long to learn that getting approved for Social Security Disability is a long process; it can take almost two years.

Within a few months I got a letter of denial. Part of the letter stated, "You are too young and smart to get on disability."

I didn't want to get on Disability, but there are many people with MS under forty.

Then I received a letter from Disability Insurance, "We can get you an attorney to assist you in getting Social Security Disability." My attorney's office responded, "We are already representing Vicki Young in her appeal for Social Security Disability."

My disability insurance wanted to help me apply because once I got Social Security benefits then I would be required to repay them the majority of what they had paid me. That is the guideline for most long-term disability insurance plans.

I appealed the denial. They wanted to know details of what I did during the day. At that time, I was resting every hour or so for ten minutes. I tried to do a little bit of housework, crochet an afghan, read, or watch a little TV. Most Sundays I only went to one or two hours of my three-hour church, and typically I only drove just short distances.

When I appealed that time, they set up an appointment for me to see a psychologist. From her office I received a form to fill out with a lot of questions about my health throughout my entire life. When I met with her, one of the questions that she asked me was, 'Who was Catherine the Great?'

Really?

I don't know why they sent me to a psychologist. I would have thought they would sent me to a different neurologist.

I still didn't get approval.

The next step was to present my case before a disability law judge.

In May 2008, I got a letter that was to appear before the judge in a Salt Lake Courthouse in July.

The morning that I was to appear before the disability law judge, I got to the courthouse half an hour early as requested. I met my attorney and we looked over the paperwork from my neurologist and other medical professionals.

My attorney told me, "It's normal for the judge to be running behind." We waited about two hours.

The judge went over my information then he asked my attorney a few questions. Then the judge said to me, "I know that it can be hard to have Multiple Sclerosis. I approve you for Social Security Disability."

Afterwards, my attorney told me, "I knew he would approve you when he didn't ask you any questions."

In August 2008, I got a large check from Social Security back dating to August 2006. My attorney's portion had already been taken out. Within a few weeks, my disability insurance let me know how much I needed to pay back to them. Then, I started to receive Social Security Disability payments. I was also sent a payment from my disability insurance. It was about a fourth of the amount that I had been getting from them.

I received a letter from Social Security stating, "Your Medicare will start February 1, 2009. My Medicare card arrived at the end of October. Then in December, I signed up for a Medicare Advantage plan to be effective for February 1, 2009.

Avonex

When I first saw Dr. F, he told me that I should take Avonex, because it's better for people like me who have spinal lesions.

"Avonex is a medication manufactured by a biotechnological process from one of the naturally occurring interferons, a type of protein. It is made up of exactly the same amino acids, major components of protein. as the interferon beta found in the human body." (National MS Society's website)

I started taking Avonex in May 2006; like Copaxone, it was shipped to me.

Avonex is injected once a week into the muscle on the top of the thigh. Unlike Copaxone, there isn't an auto-injector. A nurse came to my place to show my roommate and I how to do the injections. She brought an orange to practice on.

"I have been injecting myself for over fourteen months," I told the nurse. "I can do this new medication." I injected the Avonex into my thigh, with no practice on the orange.

A major side effect Avonex is known for is flu-like symptoms, such as tiredness, chills, muscle aches, and pains, usually right after the injection, and could sometimes last for a few days.

The guidelines are to go at least four days between injections. So, if you change the day, After a few weeks I decided to do my inject on Sunday. My hands were starting to get shaky, making it hard for me to inject it, so my nurse friend, Bonnie would come over and do it for me. We were visiting teaching companions at church, so sometimes, we would go after my injection.

I took Avonex for seven months. I didn't have the side effects of chills and muscle aches and pain but I sure had a lot of fatigue; and it got progressively worse.

Tysabri

Dr. F explained, "Tysabri is a good medicine to combat your fatigue and slow down the disease progression." I decided to try it.

I started taking Tysabri in early January 2007. The guideline for taking this prescription is that you need to stop taking another disease modifying medication four weeks before starting Tysabri, so I stopped taking Avonex in early December 2006.

The chemical name for Tysabri is Natalizumab. Tysabri is an IV medication, administered in the doctor's office every four weeks. It is a *"laboratory produced monoclonal antibody. It is designed to hamper movement of potentially damaging immune cells from the bloodstream, across the blood brain barrier into the brain and spinal cord."* (NMSS website)

A very important fact to know about Tysabri is that it increases a person's risk of getting a rare brain infection that usually leads to death or severe disability. This infection is called progressive multifocal leukoencephalopathy (PML). PML usually occurs in people with a weakened immune system. Because of this severe side effect, Tysabri was taken off the market for a few months and then it was put back on with strict guidelines before I started taking it.

On November 29, 2006, I had an MRI just before I started taking Tysabri.

The first time that I went to get my infusion, the nurse asked me, "Did you read the booklet about this medication?"

"Oh, no I read as I was learning about Tysabri but I didn't realize that I was supposed to read it before the injection."

"Yes, you need to read it before," the nurse said.

Ugh, I didn't like reading. Especially an eleven-page booklet telling about PML and all of the other side effects of Tysabri. But I did before I got the first shot.

Each trip to the infusion center, a nurse took my vital signs, a few times my temperature was a little high. They waited a for my body to cool off from being outside and then they took my temperature again and it was lower, within the guidelines.

My temperature always seemed to run a little high then. Now, when I have taken my temperature when I am healthy is a low 97.4 F. I never got sick right after taking Tysabri, but there were a few times that I had to put off taking it because I was sick.

The last time I had a flu shot was before I started taking Tysabri. I was told, "Do not get a flu shot while taking Tysabri." When I started learning about holistic approaches to health, I learned that vaccines could cause autoimmune disease. I also learned and how to build up my immune system.

As part of taking Tysabri, I met with Dr. F or one of his Nurse Practitioners every three months and I had an MRI of the brain every six months.

The infusion lasted seventy minutes. When finished, then a nurse would take my vital signs. I would stay another hour in the infusion center and my vital signs were taken again to make sure that I wasn't experiencing any side effects of the medication.

While I was getting the infusion, sometimes I would sleep or read. What I liked doing most was visiting with other people who were there for the same thing. Some people would drive from surrounding states, such as Idaho or Wyoming. Jenny, one of my new friends was taking Tysabri at the same time as me. We scheduled our appointments at the infusion center at the same time so that we could visit.

Changing to a Holistic Lifestyle

"Let food be thy medicine and medicine be thy food."

– Hippocrates

At the beginning of 2009, I started going gluten free. I had read that this type of diet is good for people with auto immune disease.

For a long time, I didn't eat any bread at all, I would eat flax seed crackers. Now I eat Ezekiel bread which is sprouted grain bread and free from glyphosate. Sprouting the wheat takes away most of the gluten and the other grains in it are gluten free. I also sometimes eat sour dough bread, which has become really popular in the past six years.

I have a cousin who has Celiac, I was spending a lot of time with her then, helping with her son who was in Primary Children's Hospital. I went with her to a store that only had gluten free food. I was surprised to see gluten free vitamins there,

I asked her, "So that means that some vitamins have gluten in them?"

"Yes, because gluten is a binder." Wheat is in a lot of candy. They had a lot of gluten free candy in that store. When I get a treat, I make sure that it is free of all of the major allergens, which includes wheat and dairy.

For people with celiac, gluten free bread is made in a dedicated facility, at home they need to keep their bread away from bread that has gluten in it and use a separate toaster for their gluten free bread.

There are many people nowadays that don't have celiac but are sensitive to gluten. I know of people who are gluten sensitive, or even have Celiac disease, when they go on vacation in Europe then they are able to eat the bread there without any problems because their wheat doesn't have glyphosate in it, which is residue from weed killer. You can google glyphosate free bread to get in the United States.

In June 2009, I met with my nurse practitioner and told her, "I have been taking Tysabri for two and a half years. I'm not feeling any better than I was, sometimes I feel worse. This is not working for me, so I'm going to make a big change. I am going to stop taking Tysabri and all other medications and go on a vegan diet."

The nurse was surprised, "Wow, that is a big change. I don't know what Dr. F will think about that. Let's get you an appointment to meet with him." She scheduled it for September.

I had been taking Provigil for two and a half years to alleviate my fatigue. I was taking a higher dosage than most people and it still wasn't seeming to help. I didn't know of anything that I could take to replace it. I just continued to rest for five to ten minutes nearly every hour.

I had been taking either Tylenol or Ibuprofen at bedtime

to help control my pain so that I could sleep. I started deep breathing and using imagery. I knew that with God's help I could work through the pain and get some sleep, which I did.

By the time I met with Dr. F I was feeling a little better. I wasn't in so much pain and my last MRI showed no new lesions. Dr. F was okay with my new diet and agreed that fruits and vegetables are anti-inflammatory.

I stopped taking medications for migraines.

I did a lot of studying to change to a holistic lifestyle and I feel like this is what God inspired me to do. Many religions have dietary codes that are very similar.

Jews have dietary laws that are found in Deuteronomy and Leviticus in the Old Testament. Only kosher animals can be eaten which are mammals with split hooves and that chew their cud, such as cows and sheep. Seafood must have fins and scales and only clean birds such as chickens, ducks and geese, turkeys and pigeons are permitted. Animals must be slaughtered in a specific way to minimize suffering.

Daniel and his friends had a strict diet. The Old Testament in Daniel 1:12, says they ate pulse and drank water. Scholars have learned that their diet of pulse includes fruit, vegetables, grains, nuts and seeds.

The Seventh day Adventist diet is plant-based that empha-sizes whole food and very little meat. There is a group of Seventh Day Adventists that live in Loma Linda California. They form the only blue zone in the United States, there are four other throughout the world which is an area whose people live an average of at least ten years longer than other groups. They live a healthy lifestyle. All of the five blue zone groups eat a plant-based diet.

The Church of Jesus Christ of Latter-day Saints has the Word of Wisdom, in which the Lord declared fruits and wholesome herbs, including vegetables, should be used with prudence and thanksgiving. The "flesh of beasts and the fowls of the air should be used sparingly." Doctrine and Covenants 89:11–13

I realized that my diet needed to be as strict as Daniel's in order to heal me.

In June I started to eat mostly vegetables, fruits and grains. I ate very little meat and I just had dairy if it was an ingredient in a dish. To give my family and friends time to adjust to my new lifestyle, I told everyone that on August 1st I was going off of all animal products. It wasn't hard for me to stop eating meat. I never liked to see all of the fat that came off meat. I began eating less ice cream over a few months, which was my favorite dairy food.

I would feel a lot of pain and nausea and then eating a little food would help me feel better. The biggest change that I experienced immediately upon going on my whole food plant-based diet is that I no longer had the gastrointestinal pain that I had been suffering from for nine years.

In 2003, I changed primary care physicians. My new doctor said, "I think you're having gallbladder pain. I will order a Hida scan for you that will show the functioning of your gallbladder and any blockages."

I got the Hida scan. It uses an injected chemical to show the bile through the liver and gallbladder. The scan showed that my gallbladder was functioning at just thirty percent capacity. My understanding was that the pain I was feeling was from my gallbladder trying to work but not being able to. My primary care physician and the surgeon that she referred me to said that I should have surgery immediately, which I did.

Before the surgery, I asked the surgeon to save my gallstones. Afterwards he told me that there were no gallstones. I now had no gallbladder, but I continued to have pain. If I knew then what I know now, I would have changed my diet first, then do a cleanses to clean and strengthen my gallbladder.

About the time that I was diagnosed with MS, I started getting urinary tract infections every few months. After I changed to a whole food plant-based diet, I haven't had any more of those.

My whole food plant-based diet helped me to breathe better. In 2002, I was diagnosed with asthma. For many years I was using an inhaler to prevent an asthma attack. In the wintertime, especially, I would have a hard time breathing. When I stopped eating dairy products I stopped having asthma. I also stopped getting sick as often.

For several years, I suffered with bronchitis every winter. I don't get bronchitis anymore. Dairy is known to be mucus forming, which plays a big part in asthma and other respiratory disorders.

My skin cleared up, I didn't have adult acne anymore. I loved getting compliments from people on how good my skin looked.

When the Student is Ready the Teacher Appears

I had been inspired to go on a whole food plant-based diet and read a little bit but there was so much that I didn't know. I wanted someone local to guide and teach me about this new lifestyle. I didn't know anyone who ate a vegan diet.

In July 2009, I was in the Sunflower Farmers Market store in Murray, Utah. I noticed a sign that Vicki Talmage was going to be teaching a raw food class at their store in August.

I went to that class, and Vicki Talmage became my mentor. She was a lifestyle management coach and a colon therapist. She was healed from cancer with a raw vegan diet. She taught, "Eat a deep leafy green salad for lunch and dinner to help lessen cravings for processed food. Raw foods are living foods.

Deep leafy greens are kale, chard and collard greens. Their strong taste comes from the protein that is in them. Some leafy greens have had the protein taken out of them. Americans have been taught that we get our protein from meat and that vegetarians are deficient in protein.

When I get asked "How do you get your protein?"

I tell them, "From all the foods that I eat. All vegetables have some protein. Kale, chard and collard greens are great sources. We do not need as much protein as we have been taught. As long as a person eats enough calories, he or she will get enough protein from eating vegetables, grains, nuts and seeds.

Vicki Talmage also recommends doing cleanses every quarter. Her cleanses consist of eating watermelon for breakfast, and a big leafy green salad with cooked beets for lunch and dinner. Eat as much as you like. These foods are very cleansing. She also suggests taking cleaning supplements. When you're doing your quarterly cleanse, she recommends getting a colonic every week for two to three weeks.

A colonic is a natural way to clean the colon. During the cleanse, the colon therapist inserts a tube into the rectum while you lie on a table. A large amount of water is pushed through the tube to flush out the colon.

People have healed from many chronic diseases using colonics. I tried colonics and other times I would eat the cleansing foods of watermelon for breakfast and the salads for lunch and dinner and skip the colonics. Doing these cleanses assisted my body in the healing process.

Vicki Talmage recommends drinking two ounces of wheat grass juice every day. A superfood, wheatgrass juice contains iron, calcium, enzymes, magnesium, phytonutrients, 17 amino acids, vitamins A, C, E, K and B complex, and Chlorophyll. The chlorophyll in wheatgrass juice aids in the removal of toxic substances. Wheatgrass juice has high level of enzymes that aid in digestion as well as metabolism. It is a nutrient dense food that helps you feel fuller faster. It also enhances the function of the immune system.

I was eating better and I started to have more energy to do things.

In December 2009, I started taking Dr. Christopher's Family Herbalist class. His book, Herbal Home Health Care is the text. This is the first class in Master Herbalist Program. He started The School of Natural Healing in 1953 and Dr. Christopher was one of the few people to teach about natural healing at that time. Now there is more of a movement to go back to those simple practices of using herbs and nutritious food to build up our bodies.

On January 1, 2010, I drove the hour to my parents' house. It had been over three and a half years since I had the energy to drive all the way up to their place. Most of the time I would drive part way, they would meet me and my dad would drive my car the rest of the way. I was so excited that I had the energy to drive all the way by myself. I didn't tell them that I was coming. I was going to call them when I was just four miles away to say, "Come meet me, but no you don't need to, I am just four miles away, at the church." But then my cell phone wasn't working when I tried calling them. They were surprised to see me.

For my birthday in February 2010, my sister-in-law, Charity said, "I will come and get you and Susan and go to the Sandy Sweet Tomatoes for your birthday." That sounded good to me. I thought that there might be other family members meet us there. I was surprised that not only my parents, my brothers and sisters and their families, but also an uncle and an aunt and my friend, Bonnie. It was fun to see everyone. Sweet Tomatoes was an all you can eat buffet restaurant, with a lot of vegan options.

In March 2010, I went to the Grand Canyon with my cousin. I packed a bag with my food, fresh fruits, and vegetables. We spent time with her son, who was working at a cafeteria there. We hit a big snow storm on our way and there was a lot of snow in the Grand Canyon. It was a lot colder than I thought that it would be for March, but I did enjoy the tours.

Packing my food to take with me was a lot better than packing an auto injector and Copaxone, like I did when I visited my cousin in Los Angeles in 2005. My natural lifestyle is better than taking an injectable medication and I feel a lot better without it.

Medical doctors say that there are incurable diseases such as Multiple Sclerosis and cancer. Dr. Christopher believed that there are no incurable diseases, only incurable people. Some will not be cured of their disease, for instance, if it is their time to die.

In August 2010, I had been on my whole food plant-based lifestyle for a year so I did Dr. Christopher's incurables cleanse. I didn't have anyone to help me with it and it was complicated to do it on my own. So, I didn't do everything as outlined but it still really benefited me.

I was on this cleanse for three weeks. I drank just one type of juice each week. First I drank carrot juice second I drank apple juice, and third I drank grape juice. If I was hungry towards the end of the day then I could eat a carrot when I was drinking the carrot juice, eat an apple when I was drinking the apple juice and eat some grapes when I was drinking the grape juice. I drank close to a gallon of juice a day, a gallon of steam distilled water a day, and I took herbal supplements. The Dr. Christopher's herbal combinations that I took were Complete Tissue and Bone, Blood Stream Formula, the Lower Bowel Formula, the Nerve Formula, the Pancreas Formula, and the Herbal Calcium Formula.

I sunbathed each day in my swimsuit. The first day I stayed in the sun for two minutes each on my back and my front. Day two, I sunbathed for four minutes on each side, increasing the time by two minutes a day. That way I didn't get sunburned but I enjoyed all of the healing effects of the sun.

I went for walks, especially uphill. It helps in cleansing toxins from the body.

Some people stay on the extended cleanse for six weeks or more. I decided that three weeks was good for me. During that time, I concentrated on rebuilding my health. I wasn't doing anything else. Dr. Christopher says that when you go on a cleanse, your body lets go of all of the waste and you lose weight, most people lose more weight than is good for them and then their body stabilizes to a good weight.

I got down to one hundred seven pounds, which is too thin for me. My roommate says that I looked the worst at the end of that cleanse. But in a few weeks my weight stabilized at one hundred twelve pounds and I stayed there for many years, which was a good weight.

My Whole Food Plant Based Diet

Americans are so steeped in eating meat and dairy that it can be hard to see that there is enough variety of food to eat excluding these. I have discovered new foods such as flax seeds, chia seeds and quinoa. Sushi has become popular recently and many places with sushi have vegan sushi, which has avocado and vegetables in it. I also developed a liking for seaweed salad.

For Breakfast, I often have a green smoothie which consists of apple juice, kale or other greens, a frozen fruit blend, and a blend of berries. Other mornings, I will have strawberries, blueberries, a banana with granola and almond milk. In the summer time I like to have watermelon for breakfast.

Berries have many benefits. They have antioxidants, and different types of berries are good in strengthening the heart and preventing cancer. Cranberries and blueberries can prevent urinary tract infections. I learned many years ago that berries are good in strengthening the brain and assisting in memory. When I eat berries, I like to think that I am eating super food for my brain.

Ice Cream for breakfast! Excitement was in the air that morning. The children all had the same idea, "Let's have ice cream for breakfast."

"Sounds fun," I agreed, because we had done this before.

Six-year-old L put the apple juice in the blender.

I held up my hand. "Okay, that's good, we don't want too much, we want it to be thick." I added a handful kale.

Nine-year-old C was in charge of frozen fruit. A bag of mixed berries; blueberries, blackberries and raspberries. She also got out the frozen bag of pineapple, strawberries, peaches, and mangos.

"I want to help," said four-year-old K.

I pulled the Vita Mixer out of the cabinet. "Okay, here's the scoop to get the berries out."

K carefully put the mixed fruit and banana in the blender.

"Very good, K. You did a good job at that."

I clapped my hands together. "Time to start the Vita Mix!"

"Wait," K hurried to the other end of the house.

I knew the blender was way too noisy for her.

C turned the blender on. She held onto the lid until the mix was the perfect consistency just like I taught her.

I scooped the ice cream in bowls and we all enjoyed eating it.

When I took K to daycare that morning she told her teacher, "We had ice cream for breakfast."

I laughed. "Yes we did. Otherwise known as a green smoothie."

Sometimes I soak flaxseeds all night with raisins, walnuts, and almond. Then have that for breakfast.

Flaxseed has been grown since the beginning of civilization. It is a good source of protein, fiber and omega 3 fatty acids. For those of us who do not eat fish, flaxseeds can be our greatest source of omega 3 fats. They are a rich source of alpha-linolenic, (ALA) a plant-based omega 3 fatty acid. ALA is one of the two fatty acids that we need to obtain from the food that we eat.

We can purchase Acai bowls from several grocers, most have a health food isles, and also at health food stores. The bowls might include blueberries, strawberries, bananas and granola. Sometimes when I want to get something for breakfast that doesn't require any preparation, I pull one of those from the freezer.

For lunch and dinner, I typically have a kale salad with broccoli and cabbage. Sometimes I will have a little bit of quinoa or rice with it, or maybe black or vegetarian baked beans. There are a lot of Mexican and Chinese dishes that are vegan or we can easily prepare them ourselves without the meat.

In the winter I eat a lot of soup. Make a large pot of vegetable soup with potatoes, broccoli, cauliflower, carrots, and onions. Another good one is cauliflower soup, with blended cashew to make it creamy. When it's cold out I enjoy yams and squash.

When we don't have the time or energy to make our own food, there are a lot of prepared whole plant-based foods available now. One brand is Amy's soups and meals. Some of my favorites are lentil vegetable soup, minestrone soup, quinoa, kale and red lentil, and split pea soup. Her meals include enchiladas,

Pad Thai, tofu scramble, Thai red curry, and veggie load meal.

Avocado became a favorite food of mine when I changed to a vegan diet. It is a unique fruit, that contains a lot of heart healthy monounsaturated fat that can reduce LDL or bad cholesterol and boost HDL or good cholesterol. An avocado is full of potassium, vitamins E, A, K and B.

Avocados go with almost everything. Mexican, Chinese, always good with a salad, and they go great with breakfast either whole or in a smoothie. Avocados are a good first food for babies, too. I have given avocados to babies that I have helped raise, and they loved them.

I choose to eat half an avocado every day.

I love to have lots of fruits, vegetables, and nuts, to choose from for snacks. I keep grapes, apples, carrots, celery, cauliflower, broccoli, a variety of nuts with raisins, and gluten free crackers with hummus.

Freeze dried food is another great snack or added as part of a meal. I keep a supply of freeze-dried pineapple, apples, peaches, raspberries, strawberries, and blueberries. It's nice to just open a can and snack. Freeze dried peas, corn, spinach, broccoli, zucchini, mashed potatoes, onions, mushrooms, and tomato powder are good to have on hand and the precut onions are ready to put in recipes.

When I buy mushrooms from the store, it's hard to get them to stay fresh for a few days. Freeze-dried vegetables don't go bad, they will stay fresh if they're used within a week or two or keep them stored for twenty years. This is the best food storage for vegetables. We can open a can, rehydrate them, and the nutrients in them are like fresh vegetables.

Eating Out on a Whole Food Plant-Based Diet

There are more restaurants now than there were sixteen years ago who cater to people who eat a whole food plant-based diet or have a good selection of food. Chinese, other Asian, Mexican, and Indian restaurants, have vegan dishes. There are also soup and salad places such as Zupas and Zao's.

In Utah one of my favorites is Ginger's Garden Café, which is part of Dr. Christopher's Herb Shop in Springville, Utah. Their portabella sandwich is the best. Another favorite restaurant is Vegan Bowl in West Jordan. I'm looking forward to trying out Aubergine Kitchen. They serve fresh, nutrient dense meals made with real whole ingredients. There are several locations in Utah.

When I eat out at a high-end dining place, if I tell the waiter, "I am vegan; I would like a vegetable dish."

The waiter will bring me a plate with mushrooms to substitute for meat and a leafy green salad with lots of vegetables.

When I go to a new place I ask, "What do you have that is vegan, with no meat, no dairy or eggs. Most places have a few selections for someone on a vegan-whole food, plant-based diet, but I have been to burger places where they don't offer anything on the menu for vegans.

At one burger place the serve said, "We don't have any vegan dishes, but let me see what I can do for you." After consulting with some others, he offered, "We can make you a lettuce wrap with the veggies that we put on our burgers."

"That will be good. How much will that cost?"

The server smiled. "I don't know, I haven't done this before." He left and returned with his manager.

"This isn't something that we typically make," said the manager. "So, we'll give it to you free this time."

Two of my brothers and their families took me out to Guru's for my birthday, a fun restaurant in Provo. Guru's seemed to have a little bit of everything; pasta, bowls, soups, tacos, burritos, and pizza. They have a huge variety; I choice a Thai dish.

Whether I'm buying food at the grocery store or eating out, I'm not always able to get the best organic fruits and vegetables. I say a silent prayer that the food with be the best that it can be nutrient wise and that there won't be any bad effects of pesticides.

Kale is a super food, packed with nutrients, it has become more popular in the past fifteen years when people began adding it to green smoothies. Also loaded with beta carotene, the precursor for vitamin A. One cup of kale contains over two hundred percent of the Daily Value (DV) for adults. Vitamin A is good for the eyes, anti-inflammatory, and strengthens the immune system.

One cup of kale provides contains over eighty percent of the DV for vitamin C. It is the best-known antioxidant vitamin, helping with wound healing, and boosts the immune system to tackle colds and influenza. Kale is also one of the richest sources of Vitamin K, providing over six hundred percent of the DV. Vitamin K helps blood to clot normally.

Fiber gives structure to food, it is found abundantly in vegetables. One cup of kale contains 1% of the DV of fiber. It diminishes food cravings and gives a sense of fullness so that we will not eat more after we are full.

Quinoa, originated in the Andean region of South America,

Peru, Bolivia, Chile and Ecuador. The Incas called it the mother of all grains. Quinoa was rediscovered by the world in the late twentieth century and it has become known as a super food. It is a complete protein, containing all nine essential amino acids. With its higher protein and fiber, it aids in blood sugar management.

I like to use quinoa instead of rice when I make bowls. I combine quinoa with kale, beets, bell peppers, cucumbers, beans, and other vegetables. In Utah, Zupas restaurant makes good bowls with quinoa.

Pineapple contains a compound called bromelain, which reduces inflammation.

Tomatoes are known for the phytonutrient, lycopene. It is the pigment that gives them their red color. Lycopene is an antioxidant. It has health benefits such as protection from sun burn, heart health, and protection against certain types of cancers.

Iron

A lot of people say that they have a hard time getting the iron that they need on a vegan diet. I was always anemic or borderline anemic before I went on a whole food plant based- vegan diet. I would eat the supreme, meat lovers pizza, not because that is what I loved the most but so that I would get the iron that I needed.

I took iron pills that my Primary Care Physician recommended. I don't know if they did much for me. The iron pills seemed to go right through me, leaving my bowel movements black.

When I started on a vegan diet, I learned that there are a

lot of plant foods that are iron rich. Spinach is rich in iron. I remember watching Popeye the Sailor Man having great strength from eating spinach. Kale is another leafy green that is a good source of iron. Red vegetables such as beets, black beans, chick peas, cashews, dark chocolate, and quinoa are all good sources of iron. One of the best plant-based sources of iron is black strap molasses. One tablespoon of blackstrap molasses gives you twenty percent of your daily value for iron. Now I easily get the iron that my body needs.

You can boost your body's ability of absorbing iron by eating foods rich in vitamin C along with the iron rich food. Foods which contain fifty percent or more of vitamin C per serving- are papaya, bell peppers, broccoli, Brussel sprouts, strawberries, pineapple, oranges, kiwi, cantaloupe, cauliflower, kale, cabbage, bok choy, grapefruit, and parsley,

Think about some ways you can increase your iron intake.

Calcium

Americans have been taught for one hundred years that we need to drink milk in order to get the calcium that our bodies need. Americans drink the most milk yet we have the most cases of osteoporosis than anywhere else in the world. When we drink milk or eat dairy products we get a lot of animal protein along with the calcium. However, the animal protein prevents a lot of the calcium from milk from being absorbed by the body.

All unprocessed plant foods have good calcium content, bok choy, turnip greens, collard greens, kale, romaine lettuce, and tofu.

Vitamin B12

A nutrient that vegans can have a hard time getting is Vitamin B12.

Vitamin B12 is synthesized by bacteria, so it is naturally found in meat and dairy products. It helps keep blood cells and nerves healthy; low levels of vitamin B12 can lead to a type of anemia.

I get my vitamin B12 from nutritional yeast, which is a deactivated yeast. It contains several other B vitamins, including B1 (Thiamin), B2 (Riboflavin), B3 (Niacin), B6 (Pyridoxine), and B9 (Folate). Nutritional yeast consists of yellow flakes and has a cheesy flavor. I use it as a topping for salads and soups, and as an ingredient in recipes for non-dairy cheesy potatoes and dips.

If you want to improve your diet but do not feel like you can start eating vegan whole food plant-based diet right away, here are some things to improve your diet. Stop drinking soda pop, eating or drinking food that has artificial sweeteners, high fructose corn syrup, and other processed sugars. Cut out artificial flavors and genetically modified food.

Soda pop with or without caffeine has no nutritional value. Drinking it has several detrimental effects to your health. The sugary drink can lead to tooth decay, contribute to diabetes and heart disease.

Years ago, I read a story of a lady, we'll call her Jane, whose health started to deteriorate all of a sudden. She started to have balance issues, was having a hard time walking, losing speech and other abilities. Her doctor was wondering if she had Multiple Sclerosis. In a matter of a few weeks, she went from being normal to having a hard time functioning. Her health was deteriorating quickly.

Her sister, we'll call her Ann, read an article that drinking a lot of soda pop can have this type of effect on some people. She knew Jane drank a lot of soda pop, so after reading the article Ann called her. "What are you doing?"

"I'm about to drink a soda," said Ann.

Jane told Ann to set it down and to not drink any more.

She did.

Ann didn't drink anymore soda, and her health started to improve until it was back to normal.

Personally, I have never drank a lot of soda pop. Before I changed to a natural lifestyle, I was drinking less than ten cans of soda pop a year. I would just have a Sprite with a migraine to control the nausea. I haven't had a can of soda pop since 2008.

Interestingly, a few years ago I met a man who avoids soda pop to combat issues with heart disease.

Building My Immune System

Since I have an auto immune disease, it is important for me to build up my immune system. It has been especially important since the start of the COVID 19 pandemic. Every day I intentionally do things to strengthen my immune system.

Most days I take one or more cloves of garlic in honey or I put garlic in a salad. Garlic is the most powerful natural anti-bacterial, anti-viral and anti-fungal agent. Three cloves of garlic are equal to a dose of penicillin.

Onion is related to garlic. It has phytochemicals and vitamin C to improve immunity, chromium to assist in regulating blood sugar, and quercetin, a flavonoid, which prevents cancer, helps control blood sugar, and alleviates allergies.

It is good that we make salsa, in the Autumn, the beginning of the cold and flu season, since it is made with herbs that build the immune system.

Vitamin C builds up the immune system. Many vegetables are rich sources of vitamin C. Some alternative medical practitioners give Vitamin C IVs when people are sick.

I have been the recipient of that.

Vitamin D is important for immune function. The best source for vitamin D is the sun. I take vitamin D supplements, especially in the winter time. Many people with autoimmune disease have taken large doses of vitamin D to reduce and even eliminate their symptoms.

I take Dr. Christopher's immuncalm. It has Astragalus and marshmallow which strengthens and calms the immune system.

Elderberry is also known for building the immune system, especially in preventing and combating cold and flu viruses. Elderberry is available in child friendly gummies as well as syrup.

I make red raspberry leaf tea, especially in the winter time to prevent and treat colds or flu. Raspberry leaf tea is also good for treating canker sores, sore throats, strengthening and toning the stomach and bowels. It is effective for menstrual problems. It is good to drink during pregnancy, as it will quiet premature labor pains and assist with having an easy delivery. It enriches the milk of nursing mothers. Raspberry has many nutrients such as ascorbic acid, boron, calcium, chromium, manganese, niacin, pectin, phosphorus, potassium, riboflavin, fiber, iron, magnesium, selenium, silica, thiamin and zinc (herballegacy.com).

N-acetyl cysteine (NAC) can help the body in many ways. NAC is a highly bioavailable form of cysteine, an amino acid our bodies uses to produce glutathione. It supports the health of cells and detox pathways with its antioxidant qualities to combat harmful chemicals. When the pandemic came in 2020, there were many articles and online discussions about the benefits of NAC to support the immune system.

Many times, when I get sick, I can work through it in twenty-four hours.

Things We Put Against Our Skin

Dr. Christopher talks about the importance of wearing natural fabrics that are made from plants and animals, which are breathable fabrics. Examples of natural fabrics are linen, cotton and wool. Linen is the oldest known fabric, made from the flax plant, it is mentioned in the Bible. Linen dresses are becoming popular.

Synthetic fabrics are man made from chemicals. Examples of synthetic fabrics are nylon, polyester and rayon. Recently, I have seen several people online say that synthetic fabrics disrupt our hormones. It is especially important that we wear cotton underwear.

I try to wear one hundred percent cotton clothes as much as I can. I can tell the difference with the breathable natural cotton shirts. Many times, there are cotton/polyester blend clothes. They are popular because the polyester with the cotton lessens the wrinkles in shirts and dresses. I like to make sure that I have clothes that are at least fifty-five percent cotton.

Our skin is our biggest organ, it isn't a barrier from the outside world like a wall, but it is a sieve, letting tiny particles get into the body, that is why some medications come in a patch. When herbalists make ointments to put on the skin, they make sure that they are high quality herbs, just as if they were being used internally, because some of the herbs will get under the skin.

Make sure that your personal care products, such as soap, shampoo, conditioner and skin care products, including sun screen, are natural. Make sure that there are no artificial colors. Get products that are paraben free. They are chemical preservatives, known as butylparaben, methylparaben, and propylparaben.

I like to use doTERRA's personal care products. I have also used shampoos, conditioners, and soap from Good Earth Markets. Tea Tree essential oil is good for the skin. Rosemary is used in shampoos, and can improve scalp, hair health, and improve circulation.

Use cleaners that are free of harsh chemicals. I like doTERRA's On Guard cleaner. Good natural dish soaps are Seventh Generation and ECOS-hypoallergenic plant powered.

Biological Dentist

Go to a biological dentist who will remove your silver or dental amalgam fillings which have a mixture of mercury and silver. These fillings have been shown to leak mercury into the body and cause auto immune problems. They should be removed carefully in a way that protects the patient, the dentist, and dental assistants.

I had one side of my amalgam fillings removed in 2010, and the other amalgam fillings removed a few years later.

Use toothpaste that is free of fluoride, a good alternative is tooth powder. There are many natural toothpaste and tooth powders that you can get at Natural Food stores.

Electromagnetic Frequency

We carry our cell phones with us everywhere. Many people us them for work, school entertainment. They are always with us, and many carry their phones in their pocket.

Scientific studies shows that radiofrequency radiations emitted from cell phones are dangerous to our health. The damage can be neurological or causing cancer and infertility.

Some ways to combat the damage from cell phones; rarely put your phone in your pocket. If you do, have it on airplane mode. Do not put the phone right up to your ear when talking on it, put it on speaker phone. There is jewelry to protect yourself from EMF radiation. I have found necklaces from a company called Harmony. There are also stickers to put on cell phones and other devices such as tablets, and computers, to mitigate the radiation coming from them.

Limit young children's use of phones, and other devises.

Nature

Spend time outside in nature every day. Being in nature is healing in many ways. The earth and sun are beneficial to our bodies and spirits.

I love to be out in nature.

Dr. Christopoher taught about releasing static electricity by walking bare foot on the grass, this allows a new electrical vibration to come from the atmosphere. This is referred to as grounding. In good weather, in the Spring, Summer and Fall, I like to go outside to do some grounding by walking barefoot in the grass for five to ten minutes.

In the past few years, I have seen a lot of people post on Facebook about the importance of grounding.

It is especially important now with all of the Electromagnetic Frequency in the air from cell phones, tablets, computers. All of our devices that keep us connected have a detrimental effect on our bodies.

After working at the computer for a few hours go outside for a few minutes to recharge. I like my computer by the window where the sun shines in.

The sun helps us with our mood—it is our main source of vitamin D. Our skin synthesizes vitamin D from the UV rays of the sun. Some people get Seasonal Affective Disorder (SAD) in the winter time. Less sunlight sets off a chemical reaction in the brain which brings on symptoms of depression.

I love to walk in nature and to notice all of the plants that God has given to us for healing and enjoyment. I love to walk in parks and find new trails. I get outside for a few minutes after working on my computer. I love to be outside in the sun.

I love to have my own garden. I love to have my hands in the dirt, planting the vegetables, taking care of them, and harvesting them.

Personally, I don't ever want to be in parts of Alaska where they do not see the sun for several weeks in the winter time. I would like to visit Alaska in the summertime and experience the nearly twenty-four hours of sunlight.

Dr. Christopher taught that we get a basis of good health through a whole lifestyle approach of a mucusless diet, herbs, and being out in nature. Do not use a particular herb in place of a particular medicine, but use certain herbs to cleanse and others to heal, etc. This is the vitalist holistic approach.

I was watching a DVD by David Christopher for one of my classes at the School of Natural Healing. He asked the students, "What is the personality of someone who has Multiple Sclerosis?"

The students didn't know.

I knew the answer.

That was one of the times that I wished I was a part of the live class.

Sitting there, in front of the screen, I raised my hand. "I know those of us who are diagnosed with Multiple Sclerosis are go getters. We have a drive to get things done, staying up late at night and then getting up early in the morning to accomplice all that we want to do. Athletes, actors, musicians have been diagnosed with MS, they are all go getters. We keep doing as much as we can before our bodies say, no, with symptoms of fatigue, foot drop, etc., but then we still try to do more."

Then I heard David Christopoher's answer, "People who are diagnosed with MS are go getters. They go and go and go until they can't go anymore. When they can't walk anymore they do as much as they can as they wheel around in a wheelchair. When they get to the point that all that they can do is lay in bed and move their eyes to read, they read as much as they can, moving their eyes back and forth on the page."

The Herb Licorice

I wrote my master's thesis on licorice. Whenever I told friends my topic, they would often respond, "I thought licorice was just a candy." Just like peppermint the inspiration for the candy came from a plant and it has many of the same medicinal properties such as assisting with digestion and giving the body energy. I chose to study licorice mainly because it combats adrenal fatigue, so it could relieve my fatigue from Multiple Sclerosis.

Licorice has been used since ancient times. It has been found in Egyptian tombs that are three thousand years old. The ancient Greeks, Romans, Babylonians and Chinese used it. The main species of licorice that we use, Glyrrhiza glabra grows in Spain, Italy, and Greece. It was brought to the United States by colonists who taught the American Indians how to use it; a switch from the Indians teaching the colonists about many plants.

Like alfalfa, the licorice plant is in the legume family. It is a graceful plant, with a feathery appearance. It has small pale blue, violet, yellowish white or purplish flowers, followed by small pods that resemble a partially grown pea pods. Like other plants in the legume family, licorice has a double underground system. The vertical tap root, penetrating three or four feet deep and a horizontal rhizomes which can grow to six feet. The root and rhizome are the parts of the plant that is used medicinally.

Licorice's main therapeutic compound, glycyrrhizin, is fifty times sweeter than sugar, yet it does not affect blood glucose levels. It is good for diabetics, and unlike other sweeteners, it decreases thirst instead of increasing it. Licorice is used for the endocrine system, respiratory system, digestion, nervous system, immune system, reproductive system and has anticancer properties.

People who drive long distances and work night shifts often take licorice extract along to stay awake and energized. This can be purchased in health food stores. Licorice gives the body nutrients and has energizing effects.

I made an herbal formula which I called Alert; it has licorice as its base. I used alfalfa for its many nutrients, especially vitamin D and vitamin B12.

Our assignment was part of my master herbalist classes through Dr. Christopher was to make our herbal formula in two forms. I chose to make mine as a tincture and capsules. After I completed the assignment, I just make it into capsules. I have also made glycerites, which is using vegetable glycerin instead of alcohol for the solvent.

An herbal tincture is made by dissolving an herb or and

herbal formula into alcohol. To make an herbaltincture, fill a glass mason jar with one-ounce dried herbs, licorice, alfalfa, and nettle, and cover with five ounces of eighty proof vodka. The alcohol helps to bring out the medicinal qualities of the herbs. Store mixture in a dark place for two weeks, shaking morning and evening. Then, strain the mixture through cheese cloth, put in dark dropper bottles, and label.

To make herbal capsules, mix the powdered herbs together, put one half of a vegan capsule in a capsule machine, pour the powdered herbs over it, use a tool to scrape all of the extra powder off. Put the other half of the capsules in the other side of the machine and then put them together. Capsule machines come in different sizes. The smallest has twenty-four holes, one that fills forty-eight capsules, and up to one hundred capsules or more. I buy the herbs and empty vegetable capsules at a health food store, and the capsule machines online.

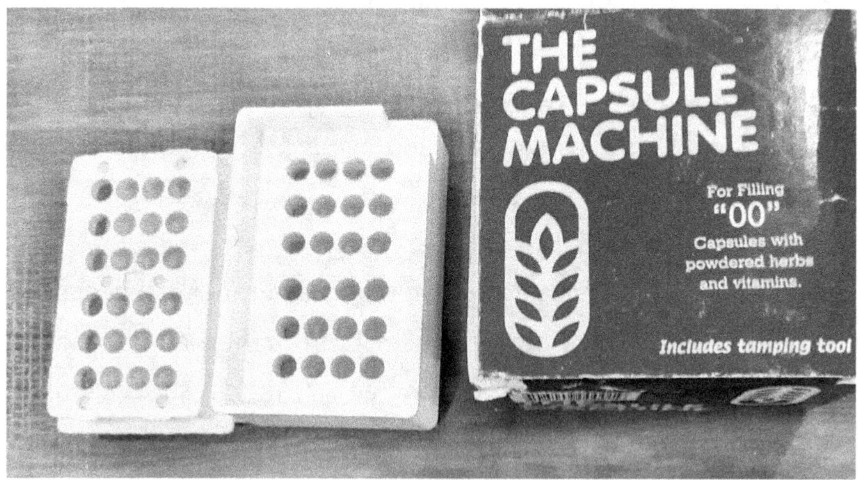

Water

I grew up in the country drinking water from a well. Many cities have chemicals added to the drinking water, including fluoride.

Dr. Christopher says to drink about a gallon of steam distilled water a day for adults.

I have been drinking steam distilled water since August of 2009. I feel best when I drink about twelve to sixteen cups of water a day.

Steam distilled is pure water with all of the impurities and minerals taken out. Steam distilled water is first turned into steam so that all of its impurities are taken away. Then, through condensation, it is turned into pure water. Rain water would be pure water if there wasn't pollution in the air. Some people say that alkaline water is better than steam distilled water.

Alkaline water is steam distilled which has had minerals added. The mineral in the water makes it alkaline. Pure steam distilled water is neutral, which is seven on the pH scale. An alkaline diet is the best for health.

I choose to drink pure natural water and my food, including fruits and vegetables are alkaline. Meat and grains are acidic. Steam distilled water is the best for making tea. Being pure water, it draws out what is needed from the herbs.

It is important to make sure that you are getting the electrolytes that you need. This helps you stay hydrated. I use Just Ingredients Electrolytes, which is just real fruit, sea salt and trace minerals. They have several different flavors. Their lemonade electrolytes tastes like real lemonade.

Dr. Christopher's Herbal Blends

Dr. Christopher's Complete Tissue and Bone ointment is used for ointment for cuts, scrapes and bruises. Use cayenne ointment, which brings blood to that area to assist in the healing process and then put Complete Tissue and Bone on top of the ointment. Many people use Complete Tissue and Bone on their knees.

When I fractured my sacrum, I healed amazingly well, and I attribute that to taking Dr. Christopher's Complete Tissue and Bone capsules. There are a lot of stories of using it to grow back a fingertip that was cut off, also amazing stories of healing using this with other formulas with a whole food plant-based diet.

I use Dr. Christopher's Immucalm with marshmallow and Astragulus. This herbal combination calms, soothes, and strengthens the immune system. It is for those with auto immune disease and allergies, it also stimulates the body's ability to fight off infection.

Essential Oils

In September 2011, Vicki Talmage introduced me to doTERRA's essential oils. I love these and have been using them ever since. I have introduced them to many people.

Some of my favorite essential oils are peppermint, lavender, frankincense, and the blends, Breathe, On Guard and Past Tense.

Peppermint helps with digestion, respiratory issues, headaches, and energy. It is in the digestion blend, respiratory and the headache blend. When I do not have blends with me, I put peppermint on my skin over my stomach to assist with digestive issues, I put a drop in my hand and breath it in for respiratory issues, and I put it on my forehead by itself or with frankincense for migraines.

Lavender is calming. It has become popular in the past few years, I love to see lavender plants around buildings in cities. Using it is a natural way to calm the body to go to sleep. I sometimes put lavender on my pillow or on my wrist at night; it is good for first aid. We use it to soothe sunburns.

Frankincense is a powerful essential oil. It soothes and calms the central nervous system so it is an important one to use in treating Multiple Sclerosis. It is an ingredient in essential oil blends to relieve headaches. Sometimes I have used peppermint and frankincense together to relieve a migraine. Frankincense is good at preventing and treating scars. When I fell and cut my chin and got stitches, I put frankincense on my chin and after a few months I did not have a scar.

DoTERRA's Breathe is a great blend to soothe the respiratory system. When I feel like I am getting a cold, I like to take a Breathe Drop, it is so refreshing and helps me feel better. I took care of one of my nephews when he was a baby and a toddler. One winter I was watching him once a week. I gave him one Breathe drop each time. He didn't get sick that winter.

A friend realized that she could take a Breathe drop every morning during allergy season and she wouldn't break out with hives, like she had in the past from the trees she is allergic to.

DoTERRA's On Guard is an essential oil blend to strengthen the immune system. Put it on the bottom of your feet during the cold and flu season to help you stay healthy. There are many different ways to use On Guard, it comes in several different forms. My mom likes to take On Guard soft gels.

Past Tense is DoTERRA's headache blend. When I start to feel a migraine, I will put Past Tense on my forehead and many times I can stop it right then. Some of its ingredients are frankincense, wintergreen, lavender and peppermint. I love the scent so I use it quite a bit. When I'm using Past Tense I'm often told, "You smell so good."

Learning From and Overcoming the Hard Symptoms

Pain

Pain stayed so long I said to him today,
"I will not have you with me anymore."
I stamped my foot and said, "Be on your way."
And paused there, startled at the look he wore,
"I who have been your friend," he said to me.
I who have been your teacher—all you know
Of understanding, love, of sympathy
And patience, I have taught you. Shall I go?"

Sometimes we get teachers that we never wanted. Pain is one of those. Over twenty years living with pain has taught me a few things.

Acute pain lets us know that we have just been injured. Our bodies are good at healing this. Then there is chronic pain. Sometimes our bodies get stuck in the pain signal and we need to figure out what we need to learn from that pain.

One morning at the MS Exercise Program I lifted a twenty-five-pound weight off a machine and accidently dropped it on my left hand. My pointer finger got most of the weight, and wow, was that painful. I cried for about fifteen minutes because it hurt so bad.

I sat down at a table and someone gave me an ice pack to put on my finger. I assured them, "I'm fine, my finger is fine, it's just that my nerve was irritated."

My finger wasn't broken, and I was fine.

Several people told me they "I wouldn't have been able to feel the pain."

Less sensitivity is a common symptom of MS.

I was grateful that I could feel the pain. When we injure ourselves, God has given us the gift of pain to let us know that there is a problem that needs to be taken care of.

In our American society, many just want to take medication or have surgery to get rid of the pain. However, if we would do more investigating to find out what is causing the pain, then we can make the changes to correct the problem.

An analogy to stopping the pain would be like stopping when the fix engine light comes on a in our car, and instead of getting to the root of the problem, we simply unplug the light.

Multiple Sclerosis pain is tingly and numb. For years I felt that my left foot was "asleep' with that feeling of pins and needles, and numbness. That was also the pain that I felt in my left wrist that would come and go.

I think that the worst pain that I have ever had was in 2015, I had pain in my chest after being sick. I had been coughing really hard and it hurt to breathe. I went to the ER and the doctor said that I might have broken a rib from coughing hard. I got x-rays which didn't show any broken ribs, so it was determined that I had injured the intercostal muscles between my ribs; these muscles help us breathe.

The doctor wanted to give me a really strong medication, like Lortab. But it had proven in the past that it doesn't work for me. He prescribed eight hundred mg Ibuprofen. I took just a few, but I mostly took White Willow capsules.

When I told Dr. F that I was taking White Willow. He said, "Aspirin is synthesized from White Willow. Wow, you went right to the source."

The hard part with this pain is that it wasn't gone after a few weeks, it was still there months later, not as bad as at the beginning but I could still feel it and sometimes it would be all around my chest and into my back. It was frustrating because I wasn't able to do all that I wanted to do. I wondered if it was caused by what is called MS hug, which is also known as banding or girdling. It's chest pain, rib pain, or a tight uncomfortable feeling, and it's hard to breathe. I hadn't had any MS relapses since I started my whole food plant-based diet in 2009. I didn't like the idea that I might have a new MS symptom but I wanted to figure out what was causing the pain.

Dr. F. ordered an MRI of my thoracic spine in March 2016. Two days later I looked up the results on the Intermountain Health Care portal. Instead of showing a new lesion, it showed no lesions in the thoracic spine. All of the lesions that I had in that area were gone.

Wow, this is the result of all that I have been inspired to do. At my next appointment with Dr. F, he gave me his perspective as a neurologist. He was surprised that the MRI scan didn't show any lesions where there had been some previously. He pointed upward. "This doesn't happen. You must be friends with the man upstairs"

Yes, God is my friend and he has helped me through this. Maybe I was supposed to get that MRI to see the miracle of no lesions on my thoracic spine.

Two nights before Christmas in 2018, I had just gotten to bed. All of a sudden I started feeling that I was being pinched on the back of my upper right leg all night long, and I hardly got any sleep. In the morning, when I checked in a mirror, I had a rash on the back of my leg. I went to an urgent care center and was advised, "You have shingles."

Father's Day 2021 was a good day. I was feeling good and had a good visit with my dad, and mom at their house. When it was time for me to leave, I got in my van and like I always do, reached up with my left hand to get my seatbelt. But this time was different. When I tried to reach up to I could hardly lift my hand because my left shoulder and upper arm were so tight and stiff.

This is strange. I haven't injured it.

I went to an orthopedic doctor who told me that I had frozen shoulder. He didn't have any idea how I got it."

I had a chiropractor tell me, "Since you have MS, you are prone to getting a frozen shoulder."

My neurologist thought otherwise.

It was soon second nature to use my right hand to reach across my body to grab the seat belt and click it. It was many little movements that became hard to do; reaching up, or back or movements that were close to my body such as reaching into pockets.

In restrooms, so often the toilet paper is located on the left, situated so that you need to reach a little behind where you are sitting. That became so awkward and hard for me to get. I would turn my body and reach over with my right hand to get it.

Getting dressed was the hardest thing to do. I went the thrift store and bought several long sleeve button shirts that were a size too big for me. It is best to avoid putting clothes over your head when you have an injured shoulder. Also, when putting a shirt or jacket on, put the injured arm in first.

I used Complete Tissue and Bone ointment on my shoulder and took ten capsules of Complete Tissue and Bone every day for a while. I also took turmeric for the inflammation.

As Halloween was coming, I was still working diligently to keep my shoulder working. I haven't been one to dress up for Halloween as an adult.

I had a joint that needs to be oiled to keep working. I feel like the tin woman.

I often wondered, how can I overcome chronic pain? What is the opposite that I can tell my body? I thought about a declaration of, I feel good. I talked to a chiropractor about how to express this.

He suggested, "A lot of people talk about being gluten free, you can be pain free."

I liked that. I don't have as much pain as I used to. Medical professionals are surprised that I healed a frozen shoulder without surgery.

Migraines

I had my first migraine when I was twenty-seven. In June of 1997, I drove my sister and four friends from Provo to the Mormon Miracle Pageant in Manti, Utah. We got there early in the evening, ate, got a place to sit to watch the Pageant, which was high on a hill. The Pageant started at 9:30 pm and lasted a little over an hour. We waited for most of the traffic to go before we headed out to a friend's parents place five miles away. The others slept outside, but I slept inside since I had a headache. The lights were bothering me, so my sister drove us back to Provo the next morning.

I had a few more migraines over the next two years, but by the year 2000, I was getting them frequently; at least two a month. When the lights would start bothering me it would feel like my eye was being bored into with pulsating pain. It was just above my eye. Most of the time it would be on my left side, or sometimes on my right side affecting that eye. Sometimes I would have nausea, and a few times I would vomit. That would relieve the nausea and then I would start to feel better. Some-times I couldn't do anything but lay in a dark room and try to get some sleep. Many times, the migraines would last for two days.

I went to my Primary Care Physician in 2000 to get treat-ment for the migraines and was given two types of medications. One every day to prevent the headaches, and the other one to stop them from getting too bad.

In 2004, my PCP referred me to Dr. L, a neurologist. He managed my medications to determine if I needed more of one medicine to get the migraines under control.

When I started going to Dr. T. for Multiple Sclerosis, he said that he could also treat the migraines. He ended up treating ed me for both.

When I started going to Dr. F., he told me that he specialized in Multiple Sclerosis and that he would refer me to Dr. D at the Salt Lake Clinic, who specialized in migraines."

Now I was going to two different neurologists.

One medication gave me the side effect of a tingly sensation in my hands. That really bothered me, because I already had that from the MS. I didn't want a medication giving me the same thing. Dr. D was good to work with me until I found natural ways to stop my migraines.

I learned a lot of people with Multiple Sclerosis had migraines.

It can be genetic and also caused by environmental factors. Migraines often run in families. My mom used to get migraines when she was younger. My younger sister does as well.

There are many different things that can trigger a migraine. Hormonal changes, sensory stimuli, stress, lack of sleep, and some foods.

For some women, hormonal changes such as before or during their menstrual periods can trigger a migraine. This hasn't been true for me. Migraines are more common in women than men.

Sensory stimuli, such as bright lights, or sunlight, loud noises, strong smells such as cigarette smoke. For me, it's bright lights. I wear sunglasses when I drive during the day. Flashing lights such as from a police car, or toys with bright lights are hard on me. I seem to be doing better; bright lights don't give me migraines any more. Strong smells can be a trigger. For a long time, cigarette smoke would start the pulsating sensation of a migraine coming on.

About nine years ago, I had neighbors who smoked. If I could smell it when I went outside I would start to feel one coming on. Then I decided that I would not let cigarette smoke bother me. I haven't gotten a migraine after smelling cigarette smoke since then.

Some foods that trigger, are gluten and cheese, chocolate, food preservatives such as nitrates, nitrites, MSG and artificial sweeteners. I stay away from these foods. When I eat chocolate, I make sure that it is high quality dark chocolate.

Fasting or going awhile without eating can cause a migraine, or when I'm dehydrated I make sure I drink a lot of water each day and when I fast I make sure I eat a big meal before I start, then it's just a water fast.

I have done a lot of things to treat migraines. I never thought that taking medication was the best thing to control these powerful headaches. I think that sometimes I was getting rebound headaches from the medicine. I have worn rose colored glasses, use relaxation techniques, chiropractic adjustments, massage, taken essential oils, and herbs.

I tried the rose-colored glasses all of the time for about two years. There are studies that have shown those glasses may help reduce migraine pain for some people. I wore a rose-tinted clip over my glasses. I didn't notice much improvement.

I sometimes do relaxation techniques and an affirmation that many times stop the migraine when it first starts to come on. Sometimes a head massage helps me to relax. My roommate

Susan gives good head massages that relieves my migraines. Sometimes I put an ice pack or anything cold on my forehead.

I have gotten NAET from a chiropractor, which stands for Nambudripad's Allergy Elimination Technique.

NAET uses kinesiology, chiropractic and acupressure to desensitize the body to allergens. By clearing energy blockages related to specific substances, NAET relieves symptoms to food and environmental allergies which relieves headaches.

I have taken half a teaspoon of cayenne in water to prevent a migraine from coming on. The cayenne works and it helps me to drink a lot of water. Drinking a lot of water helps to prevent and alleviate migraines.

The herb, feverfew is known to prevent migraines. Feverfew limits the inflammation of blood vessels in the head, thus stopping the spasms that contribute to migraines.

Falls

When I was first diagnosed with Multiple sclerosis, I was tripping and falling frequently. When I walked on tile, I felt like I was making a lot of noise. I fell several times without any injuries.

Early one Saturday morning, I fell climbing up the stairs at work. Some people in a neighboring building saw me fall and asked, ""Hey, are you okay?"

'Yes, I'm fine." I hurried on my way.

One semester I was taking an evening class at the University of Utah, it was a two-and-a-half-hour class and we had a break half way through. On one break, I was climbing a few stairs to go to the rest room and I fell again. There were a lot of people around me. I just felt embarrassed that I had fallen and that things had fallen out of my pocket.

In April 2007, I fell walking down the stairs to my apartment. I had fallen many times walking up the stairs, this was the first time I had fallen walking down the stairs. I thought my left ankle was seriously sprained. This seemed a lot worse than my past injury. My ankle was swollen so I left my shoe on to act as a splint.

I drove to an urgent care facility. When I checked in I asked, "Is there was a chair that I could sit in while I filling out the paperwork?"

A receptionist quickly brought me a wheelchair.

I sat in it the entire time. I told them, "I fell down the stairs." They took me right back. They were asking me if my back hurt or other areas of my body. I realized that they thought that I had fallen down several stairs I explained fell while walking down the stairs, not all the way down.

A medical assistant cut my sock off my very swollen ankle. When the doctor saw it he said, "It looks like you could have a broken ankle."

I didn't want it to be broken. During the x-ray. I was praying that it wouldn't be broke, that it would just be sprained.

The x-rays showed that I had sprained my ankle. Later, I was told that a sprained ankle can sometimes be worse than a broken ankle. The doctor told me that I should use a cane because I didn't have the upper body strength for crutches.

The nurse wrapped my left ankle with an elastic bandage and put a cast shoe on it. She took me out to my car in the wheelchair. She said, "I don't know if you should be driving home."

I shrugged. "I drove here and I can drive the few miles back home. I am grateful it's my left ankle, I wouldn't be able to drive if it were my right."

A friend loaned me a cane. I had to learn to walk using it. You hold the cane in the hand that is opposite the injured leg. You move the cane at the same time as the injured leg.

Now, with a sprained ankle, I felt even more fatigue. I would shower in the morning, re-wrap my ankle, and feel like I had put in a full day of work.

People from church brought me meals while I was healing. Another gave me a ride to and from the infusion center. It was a lot better than riding the bus.

With a sprained ankle, I moved less than I had been so I gained nine pounds. That nine pounds made a difference to me, I couldn't wear the size ten pants that I had worn all of my adult life, I had to get size twelve pants. It took about a year to release the weight.

I used the wheelchair carts in grocery stores for the first time. It took me awhile to get used to driving them. The wheelchair carts are also good to use in stores to help with fatigue but just holding onto the shopping cart helped me.

I got physical therapy for my sprained ankle. I did range of motion exercises and weight bearing exercises. The physical therapist laughed at how slow I was walking on my first visit. She gave me some more pointers with walking with the cane and then on my next visit she was surprised on how fast I was walking.

My physical therapist at Intermountain Healthcare told me about the Multiple Sclerosis Exercise Program at the University of Utah Physical Therapy Department. I got a referral from my neurologist, Dr. F and started going to the MS Exercise Program.

In 2008, I was going for a walk in my neighborhood and tripped and fell on the broken sidewalk. I broke my glasses and bruised my knee.

In February 2014, I fell in front of my place. I had been babysitting my nephew, his Mom came to pick him up, I went out with them and when walking back, I fell. I wish I could say that I fell on snow or ice but no, the sidewalk was clear. I think that my legs were tired and gave out. I hit my chin on the cement and felt that something was wrong in my mouth.

My sister saw me fall from her car and came to help me. I was bleeding. I asked her what it was.

"Your chin."

I put my glove on my chin to put pressure to try to stop the bleeding. My sister had an appointment so she didn't have time to help me.

I called a friend who came and took me to an Urgent Care. It was a short wait. The doctor stopped the bleeding and put stitches in my chin. He told me I should get a tetanus vaccine."

I knew the tetanus vaccine is just for prevention, not after an injury. The place that I fell was clean and I bled so I am in no danger of getting tetanus. The danger of getting tetanus is when you have a wound that doesn't bleed." I didn't get the tetanus vaccine.

After I fell, we were brushing snow with our feet to soak up my blood.

I called my dentist and got an appointment for the next day

for him to fix my chipped tooth. He said, "Eat a soft diet until you get your tooth fixed." After we left the urgent care center, we went to Zupas. I got vegetable soup to go. At home I put it in my Vitamix blender to puree it.

I got my tooth repaired the next day. He told me, "The repair is guaranteed for ten years. You should cut up apples to eat them." I followed his advice, and the repair to my tooth has lasted over twelve years. In 2024, I picked up an apple from a tree and started eating it, something that I hadn't done for ten years.

I bought big bandages to put on my chin but after trying a few sizes of Band-Aids, I found that a regular size one worked well to cover my injury. I got my stitches out a week later. Frankincense essential oil prevents scaring. I put it on my chin two or three times a day for several weeks and it healed without scarring.

After each fall, I walked more carefully, paying more attention. It took a while until I was back to having confidence when I walked and climbed up and down stairs..

In January 2017, I was leaving my parents' home after celebrating my Dad's eightieth birthday. I fell walking down their slick driveway. I was hurting so much that I couldn't move, I couldn't get up by myself. My brother and sister-in law came to help me.

It was snowing but I thought that it would be clear in a few miles. It wasn't. It was late afternoon and getting dark. I drove through the town of Wallsburg, Provo Canyon, Orem, and then onto I-15 in a snow storm. I had never driven so far in such a bad storm. I was feeling numb from the fall. I was saying a silent prayer as I was driving, asking Heavenly Father to protect me and He did. When I got on the freeway, it was hard to tell where the lanes were, there was so much snow on the road, I prayed and just followed in the tracks of the vehicle in front of me for over twenty-five miles.

When I got home, I realized how much I was hurting. I was in a lot of pain and I thought that it was my tail bone that was injured. I had heard that type of injury can cause a lot of pain even if it isn't broken. I started sitting on a pillow and even took one with me to church the next day.

I suffered with the pain for a couple of days and finally went to urgent care. I told the doctor that I had fallen on the ice.

I showed him where I hurt and he said, "That is too high to be your tail bone."

The x-ray showed that I had a hairline fracture of my sacrum, a large triangular bone at the bottom of the spine. It fits like a wedge between the two hip bones. The sacrum is made up of the sacral vertebrae, which are fused together. This was my first broken bone. The urgent care doctor didn't tell me what to do to take care of it, he gave me a list of orthopedic doctors in the county to call to set an appointment for the next day. The doctor was in Riverton, over fifteen miles from where I lived in Murray.

The orthopedic doctor looked at my x-rays. "You broke your butt bone."

He told me to rest a lot and use a donut pillow when I sit, to relieve the pressure on the tail bone, sacrum and lower back.

I was taking a lot of Dr. Christopher's Complete Tissue and Bone every day to heal. With an acute injury you can take two capsules every hour to help the body heal. When I went back to the orthopedic doctor in four weeks, he was impressed with how well my body healed.

Heat Sensitivity

A major symptom that people with Multiple Sclerosis experience is heat sensitivity.

After I was diagnosed with MS I noticed that I was more sensitive to heat in the summertime. Many times, if the temperature was over 75 F, I felt fatigue and couldn't think clearly.

One morning, in the summer of 2006, I was driving the tractor in the field, helping my dad and uncles haul hay. It was hot, the heat was hard on them too. I would drive the tractor a little ways, they would throw the hay on the wagon, then we would rest for five minutes. I would drive a little farther, they would throw the hay on, and we would rest again. We repeated that over and over until we got enough hay on the wagon to take to the barn. Then we rested in the shade and ate the granola bars.

The National Multiple Sclerosis Society provides cooling vests to those who need one. I heard about them and got a white one in 2007. I put it on over my head and it fastened on the side. It came with cold packs, which I would put in the freezer overnight and then put in the pockets of the cooling vest in the morning when I was ready to go out.

It felt and looked bulky.

I wanted to find a better option then putting on a weighted vest to help me feel cool. I wore this vest all summer when I went to the MS Exercise Program at the University of Utah.

Then one day, in September, I wasn't wearing the vest when I got on the bus.

The driver said, "Oh, I'm so glad your back is doing better, that you don't need to wear that brace anymore."

"What? Yeah my back is fine, that was a cooling vest that I was wearing to keep cool in the summertime."

In 2025, after the MS walk, I was visiting with someone who had a tan cooling vest, it looked like a regular vest and the cold packs weren't as bulky.

There are websites that sell these vests for outside workers, those with MS, and anyone who gets overheated.

I started using cooling ties in 2010. They are also called cool ties, but don't get it confused with a men's "cool" neck tie. The cool ties have beads in them that expand when they are cold. The first time I use a cooling tie I soak it in a bowl of cold water for two hours. Then after that I can soak it for just half an hour and it will keep me cool all day.

My friend Susan started making them in 2011. Cool ties have become popular. In 2025, Susan provided cooling ties for all of the children in a Liberty Day Camp.

Fatigue

Many times, in 2007-2008, I didn't have the energy to participate in three hours of church. Many Sundays, I would spend time at church resting in a recliner in the mother's lounge. Of the scripture, "see that all these things are done in wisdom and order; for it is not requisite that a man (woman) should run faster than (s)he has strength." Mosiah 4:27

It was hard to relate to other singles when I didn't have the stamina to work. What should I tell people when they ask, "What do you do?"

In 2009, I finally thought of a clever thing to say, "I conserve energy. It's a twenty-four hours a day, seven days a week job."

After taking Provigil for two and a half years, I knew in the beginning of 2009 that it was time to stop taking it. I was taking a higher dose than most people and it wasn't seeming to alleviate the fatigue. I quit taking Provigil and I didn't take any other medications for fatigue. It was time for me to learn natural ways to combat constantly being tired.

My fatigue didn't go away as quickly as I would have liked to as I was living a holistic lifestyle. In October 2013, I started taking care of my three-month-old nephew. I often took naps when he did. I would doze off a little bit when I was holding him in the recliner. I remember the first time that I took care of him, I felt energized by his spirit. I was taking care of all of his physical needs, but his spirit, like all babies, helped uplift me so I felt better.

For a while I was just resting regularly throughout the day. It helped me to close my eyes and rest for five to ten minutes every hour. I was doing this while I was taking Provigil. Sometimes I would lay down to take a nap but it was rare for me to sleep. I came to realize that even when I was so fatigued, my mind would be going over a lot of things. It took me awhile to go to sleep at night. But I knew to be energized during the day, it was important to get a good night's sleep.

One night, after having a particularly bad experience in the evening I was having a hard time going to sleep. I had just learned about declarations and I thought of one and repeated it over and over in my mind.

I am a vibrant, joyful, giving, empowering daughter of God.

I was amazed that thinking this declaration, which mentioned being vibrant, helped me go to sleep. It worked really well. I started thinking,

I am mighty strong, I am a might strong woman in Christ.

Thinking these positive thoughts were a good way for me to go to sleep.

Some nights I don't sleep very well, or I have gone to bed later and got up early. I have gone to God, saying just like you multiplied the loaves and the fishes, will you multiply my energy so that I will be able to do everything that I need to. He does multiply my energy, I have enough, I am amazed the past seven years how much he has blessed me. I have been working full time, helping to take care of children, and writing a book.

Peppermint essential oil is good to help us feel energized. A lot of times I put peppermint in my water when I am working or taking classes all day.

Cayenne is an energizing herb. Work up to taking one teaspoon of cayenne in water each day.

Staying hydrated helps us to have the energy we need throughout the day.

Many people work at a desk all day, looking at a computer and that is draining on our bodies. Just standing up every half hour helps. When you go on a break, move your body, do a little dance, go outside, feel the sun on your face.

As I have learned about my body, I have realized that sometimes when I feel fatigued, my body is telling me that it's starting to fight off a respiratory infection. So, if I rest and let myself sleep more, then I can prevent being sick. This is hard for me since I always wanting to be doing something.

In 2006–2008 I was in a book club. One month, we read the book, *The Screwtape Letters*, by C. S. Lewis. I asked the group if anyone had a book that I could borrow. Two people gave me a copy. The books were formatted differently. One of them had larger print and there was more white space on the pages. I chose that one to read. I didn't get as fatigued reading it, so at this time, I also bought large print scriptures. I didn't need glasses but reading these, I didn't get so fatigued.

*Behold, God is my salvation:
I will trust and not be afraid; for the
Lord Jehovah is my strength and my song:
he also is become my salvation.*

ISAIAH 12:2

Becoming Stronger Physically, Spiritually, and Mentally

God made our bodies to move. Exercise is important for everyone. Stretching, strength training, and cardiovascular workouts are all beneficial. One hundred years ago, many people got exercise in these areas from the activities that they did for their occupation. Now, for many of us our jobs are more sedentary so we need to make sure that we get exercise outside of our regular job.

Cardiovascular exercises include biking, running, and swimming. Biking uses different muscles than running. Swimming provides a good cardiovascular workout without putting stress on joints. Some people like to bike, others like to run or swim. I am amazed at people who do all three events in triathlons.

I need to make sure that I stretch so my body doesn't get tight. I do yoga, Pilates, and stretches to help me with running.

I went to Pilate classes that were for people with Multiple Sclerosis. These exercises are low impact. They strengthen the core, improve posture, and enhance flexibility. Pilates can be done with just a mat, or as in my specialized Pilates classes we used apparatuses. The classes were small, and the teacher moved the machine into different positions for us. Sometimes, one of my feet would spasm when I put it on the edge of the machine. I would stop the spasm by putting my foot flat on the floor.

I participated in the Multiple Sclerosis Exercise Program at the University of Utah for several years. When I started, they tested me in physical strength, stretching, cardiovascular, and balance. I was retested every year to see how I improved. They tested me on how much weight I could lift with my arms and legs, how flexible I was, all of the different muscles; my cardio-vascular endurance was tested on a recumbent elliptical cross trainer. I wasn't up to using a stationary bike and definitely not a treadmill. They also tested how fast I could walk/run a certain distance, through the halls of the building. They tested my balance by how long I could stand on one foot, and going around specific obstacles. They also tested my mental abilities with random word recall. Everything was added to my charts.

From the testing each year they customized an exercise program for me. Monday, Wednesday, and Friday from 8:00-11:00am. I was free to come in during that time and stay an hour or two, going through my assigned exercises. I would start with cardio, on the recumbent elliptical, then left weights, stretch, and go through the obstacle course, which they set up new each day.

I love to run. I was a long distant runner in high school. I ran cross country in the Fall which is a three-mile race and then I ran the mile and two-mile races in Track and Field in the Spring.

I participated in several 5K races after high school, and a 5K within a year of being diagnosed with Multiple Sclerosis. That was before I experienced severe fatigue. After a whole food plant based natural lifestyle, I got to the point where I could run again in 2011. In 2014, I was excited that I could run a 5K under forty minutes.

I ran one or two 5K races for several years. Last year, 2025, I ran a 10K in preparation of reaching my goal of participating in the Utah Valley Marathon, which I also ran in 2025. It goes past my mom's house less than half a mile from the start of the race.

It was exhilarating to be in the race after watching the runners go by for over ten years. It felt so good to be running down Wallsburg valley, down Provo canyon to University Avenue in Provo and finish by Center street. This was an area that I had driven hundreds of times, so I knew it well. It felt so good running down by Bridal Veil Falls. I finished last but I finished in less than eight hours. I felt good and amazingly the eighty-degree heat wasn't too draining. I had a cold towel on my shoulders to help keep my body cool.

Currently I go to a physical therapist/trainer who gives me tips on running. I'm encouraged to run every other day.

Managing Stress

Recently it seems like more people are stressed out. I'm always seeing heated discussions on social media, or witnessing interactions with coworkers, friends, and family.

It is important to find healthful ways to manage stress.

For many years, I have been taking ashwagandha, an adaptogen herb that helps the body manage physical, mental and emotional stress. Adaptogen are herbs that help your body respond to stress, fatigue, and overall wellbeing. Ashwagandha lowers cortisol levels and improves sleep. It may improve muscle strength, focus, memory, and support heart health. I don't take it continuously but for two or three months at a time.

I also take Dr. Christopher's Mind Trac formula for a month or two at a time. It's a formula for emotional clarity. Valerian root, and Skullcap are both nervine sedatives and antispasmodics. They calm nerves and muscles and promote restful sleep. Mullein and Lobelia help cleanse the blood. St John's Wort is an effective antidepressant. Gotu Kola and Gingko Biloba helps improve the blood flow and oxygen circulation to the head, they help improve memory, nerve response and mental alertness. A base of Jurassic Green supplies the body with essential vitamins and minerals.

At the beginning of the day, or end the day, it's helpful for me to write out frustration pages. I have heard many people refer to this as morning pages, but I like the description of frustration pages, since I am writing out my exasperations. Doing this before going to bed helps me get to sleep.

Deep breathing and meditation can help relieve stress at any time of the day.

Years ago, I did Emotional Freedom Technique or EFT, with a practitioner. I still use it to work through emotions. You tap on different points on your body and say I feel overwhelmed. Even though I feel overwhelmed, I completely love and accept myself. After I tap for a few minutes, I feel the emotion lessen.

No matter our circumstances, we can find joy in our lives.

When I purposely think in the morning, "What am I going to do to find joy today?" My day goes better. I find joy as I go for a walk, work in my garden, or help a child. I see my blessings in all of the little things as I go throughout my day finding joy.

Doing Service for Others

Everyone likes to feel needed. I have heard many stories of people, who were bedridden, but still served others by writing letters or calling them on the phone.

In 2007, a friend asked me to come to her condo while she was at work. She needed someone to be there when a repairman came to repair a leak in her bathroom. Another friend also asked me to come over while a repairman did some work in her condo. I am grateful that I could help both of them.

My cousin Emily's son, Dameon, was three and a half when he was admitted to Primary Children's Hospital in December 2008, awaiting brain surgery. He had his first surgery right before Christmas with a terrible result. When they did the surgery, he had a stroke and ended up in a wheelchair. He had a trach to help him breathe, and to receive nourishment, a g-tube in his stomach.

He required several more surgeries and was in the hospital for two and a half months. His family lived two hours away, his parents worked during the week. They tried to spend as much time with him as they could.

Monday, Wednesday, and Friday, I rode the bus to the Multiple Sclerosis Exercise Program from 8:00 to 9:00am at Research Park at the University of Utah. Then I took the bus to Primary Children's Hospital to spend time with Dameon. I stayed until about 4:00pm. His aunt and uncle would be there as well, and sometimes I got a ride home with them.

Spending time with Dameon is one of the hardest volunteer jobs I ever had. After that first surgery his body was very stiff, I wished I could just rub his fingers and help them soften. Sometimes his nurse would adjust his machines and put him in my lap so that I could hold him as I sat in a recliner. I read to him and went to physical therapy appointments with him. Other times, a music therapist would bring different musical instruments and sing to him.

His parents and aunt got trained to take care of his trach and g-tube.

When a new nurse or CNA who hadn't met me would ask, "Are you trained to take care of his trach and g-tube?"

"No, I am just here to love him."

I wished that I could have spent five days a week with him instead of just three, but it was draining on me, so I would do a lot of resting in his room.

After that long hospital stay, there were times that he would be there again for a few days or a week, and I would spend time with him then, too.

Spiritual

Each morning after I wake up, I think about putting on the armor of God, as the Apostle Paul taught in Ephesians 6:11–18:

"Put on the whole armor of God, that ye may be able to stand against the wiles of the devil.

For we wrestle not against flesh and blood, but against principalities, against powers, against the rulers of darkness of this world, against spiritual wickedness in high places.

Wherefore take unto you the whole armor of God, that ye may be able to withstand in the evil day, and having done all, to stand.

Stand therefore, having your loins girt about with truth, and having on the breastplate of righteousness;

And your feet shod with the preparation of the gospel of peace;

Above all, taking the shield of faith, wherewith ye shall be able to quench all the fiery darts of the wicked.

And take the helmet of salvation, and the sword of the Spirit, which is the word of God.

Praying always with all prayer and supplication."

I do this by scripture study, prayer, medication, song, declarations, looking at my vision board, and exercise.

This is the armor that medieval knights wore; made of metal to give the greatest protection. God protects me from the EMF and pollution of the world.

Seek and Expect Miracles

I have noticed with me, and with others, that when we seek and expect miracles, we see the hand of God in our lives, and great things happen.

Be grateful, notice the hand of God in the little everyday things and thank him. I have gratitude for the energy that I need to put in long twelve-hour work days several days in a row. Also, that my running is improving.

I'm grateful that God has healed me from Multiple Sclerosis.

Recently my niece lost her phone. We knew that it wasn't at our place, it had been missing it for over twenty-four hours, and she was upset.

I told her, "We need to be calm and have faith that it will be found."

Just then there was a knock at the door.

She opened it to a young man who said, "Here's your phone." Then he left.

It was her phone and that was our big miracle for that day.

You Need to Have a Big Why

You need to have a big why in order to change to a holistic lifestyle. I would rather have my whole food plant-based diet than take an injectable medication. But that is not what I consider all the time. What I think about is building my health. I eat well, exercise, spend time in nature, use herbs and essential oils, build myself mentally and spiritually so that I can be healthy in all areas of my life.

A few years ago, a friend with a diagnosis of Multiple Sclerosis, told me, "I'm afraid of having a relapse."

I'm not afraid of having a relapse. I have not thought about having one for many years. Every day I think about all the ways that I can stay healthy. What we think about, we get. I hope that this book has helped you realize that what you do and think has a big impact on your life. Do things and keep your thoughts on that which will move you towards being healthy.

What is one thing that you can do today that will improve your health?

A favorite scripture of mine is, Philippians 4:13 *"I can do all things through Christ which strengtheneth me."*

I know that Christ has strengthened me many times through my health challenges. As I have relied on Him, He has helped me through Multiple Sclerosis, to become Mighty Strong in Christ.

He helped me overcome my weakness of fatigue. As Ether 12:27 says, *"…my grace is sufficient for all men that humble themselves before me; for if they humble themselves before me, and have faith in me, then will I make weak things become strong unto them."*

Patience

Years ago, I had the idea of coming up with a color and an object to represent a value and what it means to me. My value is Patience and it is represented by a silver pitcher. It is filled up by challenges and then I can pour them out as I learn from them and teach others.

Malachi 3:2 says, *"And he shall sit as a refiner and a purifier of silver."*

Jesus refines us. Silver is purified when the refiner can see his reflection in it. Jesus knows the process is complete when he sees his reflection in us.

I have had a scripture posted in my bathroom for many years. *"Know ye not that ye are the temple of God and that the spirit of God dwelleth in you?"* 1 Corinthians 3:16

This scripture has helped me remember my why. I'm eating to keep my body, which is a temple, pure and healthy.

Becoming Aware of the Words We Use

Our brains hear the words that we say or think, the brain doesn't think in negatives. People might say, "Don't forget this event."

In that sentence, it seems like forget is emphasized.

Let's say the positive. "Please remember this."

When people say, "Don't forget…" to me, I say I will remember to reinforce to my brain that I remember things. People joke about growing old and not remembering things, and I have even heard people talk about getting Alzheimer's in the future.

Let's instead think I can remember things, I still remember things. My dad never talked about forgetting or not remember things and he had a great memory till the end of his life.

I was so fatigued for many years that it seemed to become who I was. I needed to change that. Instead of saying, "I am tired." I started to consciously say, "I am feeling tired right now."

It's a temporary thing. "I am feeling tired because I was working hard."

I don't want to feel all this pain that I have been having all of the time.

I should think positive.

Our body doesn't think in the negative, "I have no pain."

Instead, "I'm pain free."

My left leg is weaker than my right but thinking that thought doesn't seem to help.

A physical therapist said it like this, "Your left leg isn't as strong as your right leg."

Yes, I like saying it that way. My left leg isn't as strong, yet, but it's getting stronger every day.

It is easier to say MS instead of Multiple Sclerosis but be aware of saying MS. Many years ago, I said to a lady, "I have MS."

She said, "You have a mess?"

I said, "No, at least that is not what I was saying. I was saying that I have Multiple Sclerosis."

A friend of mine from the Multiple Sclerosis Exercise Program told me, "One time I was talking on the phone and said, "I have MS."

My four-year-old grandson overheard what I said and when I got off the phone he said, "Grandpa, if you have a mess then you better clean it up."

I decided that Multiple Sclerosis is making me Mighty Strong. As I have gone through the challenges and mess of this diseases, God is making me Mighty Strong, not so much in a physical sense, but strong in a mental and spiritual way. My mess was Multiple Sclerosis, now my message is that we can all be Mighty Strong.

One time I had some friends over for one of my healthy living classes. I introduced one of my friends by saying, "She is a member of the Mighty strong club."

Join me in becoming Mighty Strong, whether or not you have a diagnosis of Multiple Sclerosis, I ask you to join me in becoming Mighty Strong in confronting and overcoming your challenges.

Part of becoming Mighty Strong is doing a little better today than you did yesterday. Do those things to help you improve physically, mentally, emotionally, and spiritually. I have observed people that aren't working to improve themselves… they decline.

I was asked recently, "What is your advice for older people to do to stay healthy?"

My advice is to stay active. I have observed too many people looking forward to retirement but then when they retire their health declines rapidly. Some people chose to keep working after sixty-five because they feel fulfilled when working. When you retire, keep doing things physically to help you stay healthy. I like seeing older people at the Recreation Center, exercising, even though it is a struggle for them. Keep moving, as the saying goes, use it, or lose it.

Keep your brain sharp as you age. This can mean different things to different people. You can google brain exercise for seniors. You can do crosswords, word searches, and sudoku. Being physically active helps the brain by enhancing blood flow to the brain. Serve others, there are many different ways to serve and this also helps you mentally, along with socially. There are several people in my writer's group who are over sixty-five, many of them have written several books and they keep writing and contributing to help others.

Declarations and Vision Boards

In 2011, I met Kirk Duncan who taught about 3 Key Elements and declarations and vision boards. A declaration is a positive statement of belief of who we want to become. It is said in present tense so our brains can recognize that this is who we are, if we say it in future tense then we are always becoming that, we don't reach it. When I say I am calm and confident, then I can feel that now.

I learned about vision boards. Put things on your vision board that are physically and mentally challenging and also put things on your vision board, such as a minivan. A goal on my vision board that I met last year was to run the Utah Valley Marathon. Now this year, I am running it again to improve my time. Now I am getting my goal of getting my book published.

Goals

I like to make goals to improve myself. At the beginning of the year, I do go over what I want to accomplish for the year. I hear about a lot of people setting big goals on January 1, and then by February saying that goal didn't work for me. I don't think that is the way to look at it. We shouldn't expect ourselves to be perfect in meeting a goal in the first few weeks. We all have bad days and we can give ourselves grace.

"I can do better tomorrow."

We all get sick and aren't able to meet our exercise goals for a few days or weeks, when we get feeling better, we can get back to exercising.

Over the past ten years I have seen many people online choose a word or a set of words to represent what they want to accomplish or feel for the year. For this year, 2026, I had someone give me a word to represent me.

The word is celebrate.

I can celebrate more, even the little wins in life and feel dopamine, the feel-good chemical, and this will help me to accomplish more.

I can be a creator of the feelings in my home. Just like God created the earth with words, we can create our home with words. On New Year's Day 2026, I wrote four words on a paper to represent how I want my home to feel and put it near my front door. The words are:

- Joy
- Love
- Peace
- Respect

I want my home to be built on Respect. People who live in my home and visit are respectful then peace and love is always felt. When respect, peace, and love are felt then it is easy to feel joy as we work and play together. These are attributes that I am teaching children. Respect one another by speaking kindly to and about others. This is a place where we can build one another up. As Peter teaches in Galatians 5: 22–23, the fruit of the spirit is love, joy, peace, patience, kindness, goodness, faithfulness, gentleness, and self-control.

When we feel good emotions then our immune system is strengthened to keep us healthy. The opposite is true, when we feel disrespected and peace is gone, then our immune system efficiency is decreased and we get sick more easily.

I want my home to be known as a place of respect, peace, love, and joy.

What are the good feelings you want to be felt in your home?

Conclusion

Find Medical Professionals who respect your opinions.

- A good diet is a basis for health.

- God has given us plants to help us heal, learn how to use them.

- Use natural products on your skin.

- Clean with natural products.

- The sun and being out in nature has many healing benefits.

- Protect yourself from electromagnetic frequency.

- Do things that will protect your mental and emotional health including staying away from artificial colors. Do tapping. Write things out on paper to work through all of the bad emotions.

Set goals, do declarations and vision boards, what works for you to help you do a little better.

Put on the armor of God, feel God's protection in your life.

Write those words that represent how you want your space to feel and put them in a place where they can be seen.

Become a little bit better each day, become stronger in Christ.

RECIPES

Vicki Young's Broccoli Kale Salad

Ingredients:

3 bunches of broccoli	1 cup coconut
1 ½ cups walnuts	½ red bell pepper
1 bunch kale	½ cup olive oil
1 cup raisins	juice of 1 lemon
1/3 head of cauliflower	3 drops lemon essential oil

Soak the raisins and walnuts for at least an hour. Mix the broccoli, cauliflower and red bell pepper together in a bowl. Add the raisins and coconut.

Dressing: mix the olive oil, lemon juice and lemon essential oil, add to the salad, stir together. Add the walnuts to the top.

I like using red bell peppers as a contrast to the green broccoli and kale and the white cauliflower, you can use any color bell pepper.

It is easy to make more or less of a salad.

Dill Vegan Cashew Cheese

2 c cashews; soaked 2 hours
Juice from one lemon
3 T nutritional yeast
½ t dill

Drain the cashews and rinse them. Add the drained cashews to a high-powered blender or food processor, along with the lemon and nutritional yeast. Add water as needed. Add the dill towards the end, get it to the consistency of cream cheese.

Use this for a dip for vegetables and crackers.

I have been given many compliments that it tastes like a cheese dip.

My Assignment on Multiple Sclerosis and Natural Treatment for the School of Natural Healing

Multiple Sclerosis (MS) is an autoimmune disease affecting the Central Nervous System.. The immune system attacks the myelin sheath around the nerves, which produces different symptoms, depending on where the myelin sheath is attacked. Most people experience fatigue, vision problems and balance problems.

Nourishing the body may stop the progression of MS and even reverse it. The Standard American Diet is full of mucus, this diet is also inflammatory. In MS, the brain is inflamed.

People with Multiple Sclerosis should follow Dr. Christopher's Mucusless Diet. The things to eliminate from the diet are processed salt, eggs, sugar flour, mil and met. The foods to enjoy are fruits and vegetables, nuts, grains and legumes. The diet should be 5-70% raw; living food has the nutrients still in them.

Eat a lot of salads with deep leafy greens, kale, chard and collard greens. They have protein and an array of nutrients.

Nuts should be soaked to take them from an acidic to an alkaline state. Berries are great brain food. Eat ½ of an avocado daily for their beneficial fat, vitamins, micronutrients, fatty acids, antioxidants and anti-inflammatory properties.

Drink a gallon of steam distilled water a day. Our bodies are 70% water. Drinking a gallon of water a day will keep us hydrated and help our bodies perform all of the many functions that include water. Water gives us more energy..

Herbs and herbal combinations- Spirulina supports brain health, boosts energy and immunity. Bee pollen for better endurance and energy, improves immune function and lowers stress levels.

Wheat grass juice contains chlorophyll and a wide range of vitamins, minerals, antioxidants, amino acids, essential fatty acids and enzymes. A few of the benefits of wheatgrass juice are a physical and mental sense of well-being, more energy and better sleep, reduced inflammation throughout the body and increase mental clarity.

Use Dr. Christopher's Immuncalm, which soothes and strengthens the immune system.

People with MS have a personality in which they want to keep going, get something done no matter what is in the way. They draw from their energy bank until there is nothing left. They need to restore their energy banks with good nutrition and rest before they cleanse.

There are various things to do to slow down. Figure out what things in your life you can give up to concentrate on restoring your health. Rest for ten minutes every one and a half hours by sitting down, closing your eyes and breathing deeply. Mediate at least once a day. Go for a walk in nature. Walk barefoot on the grass.

As you are taking these good foods and supplements for the Central Nervous System and Immune System, let them know that you are thankful for them. As you are going to sleep, you can think, "I love you, spinal cord, brain, and immune system." As you wake up in the morning be grateful for all that you have and your health that is improving.

After you have this routine down and are feeling better, then you can go on a cleanse.

And there were some who died with fevers, which at some seasons of the year were very frequent in the land—but not so much so with fevers, because of the excellent qualities of the many plants and roots which God had prepared to remove the cause of diseases, to which men were subject by the nature of the climate.

ALMA 46:40

Handouts For Healthy Living Classes Taught in My Home

Flax Seeds

#1 source of Lignans, a plant-based phytonutrient, is high in fiber.

- Antioxidant rich
- Cardiovascular benefits
- High omega 3 fatty acid content
- Antioxidant and anti-inflammatory
- Cancer prevention

Soak whole flaxseeds overnight for a good breakfast food.

Soak ¼ c flax seeds with ¾ c water overnight, you can add it to a little oatmeal and add raisins, and berries.

Ground flax seeds make a good egg replacement.

Combine 1 T flax seeds with 3 T water and then use in recipes in place of eggs.

Quinoa

- Quinoa is a grain crop grown primarily for its edible seeds.

- Quinoa originated in the Andean region of Peru, Bolivia, Ecuador, Columbia and Chile.

- The Food and Agricultural Organization of the United Nations declared 2013 to be the International Year of Quinoa

- Benefits

- Antioxidant phytonutrients

- Quercetin

- Gluten free

- Higher fat content than wheat, quinoa provides valuable amounts off heart healthy fats like monounsaturated fats, in the form of oleic acid. It also provides small amounts of the omega 3 fatty acids, alpha linolenic acid

- Quinoa is a complete protein source. It has all of these essential amino acids

Spring Foods

- Spinach
- Alfalfa
- Onion
- Celery
- Pineapple
- Blueberries
- Raspberries
- Strawberries
- Vitamin C 113%
- The Benefits of the Sun

Herb Class

- Apple Cider Vinegar-Highly acidic properties helps it stay good and it is an excellent preservative.

- To a glass of water, add a tablespoon of apple cider vinegar and honey.

- This balances the pH in the body and builds up the friendly flora.

- Licorice is a very soothing and softens the mucous membranes of the throat and lungs while cleaning any inflamed mucous membranes. This is the reason that licorice is found in a lot of cough and sore throat preparations. It reduces the irritation in the throat and has an expectorant action. Licorice loosens the phlegm in the respiratory tract so the body can expel the mucus. For colds and flus, licorice can be combined with stimulating herbs such as cayenne and ginger.

- Horehound is in the mint family and has a bitter taste. It is an expectorant.

- Ginger is an antioxidant, immune boosting, good for cardiovascular ailments, and relieves nausea.

- Cinnamon has antioxidants, anti-inflammatory, lowers blood sugar levels, protects brain function and lowers cancer risk.

- Clove is antibacterial and an immune stimulant

WAYS TO PREVENT AND TREAT RESPIRATORY AILMENTS NATURALLY

Good Source of Vitamin C

Papaya	224%	Grapefruit	59%
Bell peppers	157%	Parsley	54%
Broccoli	135%	Turnip Greens	50%
Brussel Sprouts	129%	Beet Greens	48%
Strawberries	113%	Mustard Greens	40%
Pineapple	105%	Raspberries	43%
Orange	93%	Collard Greens	40%
Kiwi	85%	Swiss Chard	42%
Cantaloupe	78%	Tomatoes	33%
Cauliflower	50%	Lemons and Limes	31%
Kale	71%	Cabbage	50%
Bok Choy	40%	Avocado	20%
Onions	15%	Apple	11%

Take These During Cold and Flu Season

- Apple Cider
- Red Raspberry Leaf Tea
- Onions, garlic
- Spices
- Herbs, licorice, horehound, elderberry

Essential Oils That Strengthen the Immune System

- Protective Blend-wild Orange, Clove Bud, Black Pepper, Cinnamon bark, Eucalyptus, Oregano, Rosemary and Melissa Essential Oils

- Respiratory Blend – Laurel Leaf, Peppermint, Eucalyptus, Melaleuca, Lemon and Cardamon Essential Oils

Positive Attitude

Believe that you can get well in less than ten days.

HANDOUT FOR A CLASS FOR A WOMEN'S RELIGIOUS GROUP

Preventing and Treating Heart Disease Naturally

Diet: Whole Food Plant Based Diet

- Asparagus, broccoli, cabbage, cauliflower, potatoes, tomatoes

- Avocado, grapefruit, oranges, peaches, watermelon,

- Grapes

- Deep leafy greens

Herbs:

• Cayenne	Turmeric
• Hawthorne	Yoga/Meditation
• Garlic	Exercise
• White Willow	Relationships
• Feeling	

Scriptures:

- Blessed are the pure in heart. (Matt 5:8; 3 Nephi 12:8)

- They that believeth were of one heart (Acts 4:32)

- Follow the Son with full purpose of heart
  (2 Nephi 31:13)

- Sacrifice unto me a broken heart and a contrite spirit.
   (3 Nephi 9:20)

- My heart pondereth continually (2 Nephi 4:16)

- Receive these things and ponder them in your heart.
  (Moroni 10:3)

- I will tell you these things in your mind and in your
  heart. (D&C 8:2)

- Christ may dwell in your heart (Eph 3:7)

- Did not our hearts burn within us? (Luke 24:32)

'I Am' Drawings

The 'I Am' drawings on the following pages represent who I am and who I want to be. Just like the declarations say who you are and who you want to be, drawings show a visual of what we are striving for to make ourselves better.

I have invited families over to my place to draw their 'I Am' pictures with markers, crayons, and stickers. The children love it.

Drawing #1 – Fruits of the Spirit

A jar tipped over with hearts, stars, and diamonds pouring out. This represents the fruits of the spirit in Galatians 5:22-23. When something hard is happening in my life that I don't have control over, I want love, joy, peace, longsuffering, gentleness, goodness, faith, and meekness to pour out of me.

Drawing #2 – I Am A Daughter of God

I am a daughter of God. The sun gives me energy. I list attributes on the rays of the sun.

Like a caterpillar transforms to a butterfly, God helped me transform from suffering with a chronic illness on disability to being healthy and full of energy.

Now you think of something that you can draw that represents who you are and who you want to be.

I am – Daughter of God

Transformation

And Jesus increased in wisdom and stature and in favour with god and man.

LUKE 2:52

GOAL PAGES

I am giving you pages to write goals in the areas of spiritual, diet, physical exercise, and emotional/mental health.

There are examples of what to work on in each area.

God helps us in all of these areas so pray for what is best for you to start working on to improve your health.

Spiritual Goals

Write down ways to put on the armor of God

Prayer, meditation, scripture study, walk, ponder in nature

Spiritual Goals

Diet Goals

Improve diet– more fruits and vegetables

Remove food with artificial colors and flavors from diet, remove foods with sugar.

133

Physical Exercise Goals

What can I do to get more movement—walk, run, dance, swim, bike

Strength training—core exercises, exercising with weights

Remember baby steps are fine, become a little stronger each day

Emotional / Mental Goals

Journal/write out frustrations, tapping, make and then ponder your 'Who I Am' picture

Declarations/ Vision Boards

REFERENCES

National Multiple Sclerosis website:
nationalmssociety.org

Multiple Sclerosis: The Questions You Have, The Answers You Need
by Rosalind C. Kalb

Vitae Health a Better Way of Living
vickitalmage.com

Dr. John R Christopher's Website Telling About His Herbs
herballegacy.com

Dr. Joel Fuhrman Books:
Eat to Live
Eat for Life

Free from the Cage: A Guide to Take You from Overwhelmed to Peace
by Jennifer Riggs
P 56–57 Emotional Freedom Technique or tapping
jennifer-riggs.com/eft-tapping/
https://youtu.be/daN4FUs7b50

*Best Day Ever – A Little Book (from a Little Guy) with Some Big Ideas
on how to Be Happy,* by Nathan Glad

Nathan has brittle bone disease. He has great wisdom for living
a life of happiness for one so young.